The Rhythm of Us

How Groups Breathe, Break, and Come
Back to Life

Dr. Matthew C. Dunn

Fractal Praxis

First Edition

ISBN: 979-8-218-84396-0

www.livinggroups.org

Contents

Dedication

Where Everything Began

To the girls (now women) of the B.C. United Fusion "Family," and to Dixie, who coached beside me—

You taught me that groups aren't made. They're found.

For two years, we breathed as one. Not because we forced it, but because something invisible held us together before we even knew each other's names. You showed me what happens when the right nervous systems find each other at the right time—how a Tuesday practice could become sacred, how teenage girls from different schools could move like they'd been together forever, how winning mattered less than the joy of being exactly who we were, together.

You were my first glimpse of the Field. My first lesson in rhythm. My first understanding that magic can't be recreated—only recognized, honored, and remembered.

Twenty years later, I still feel our rhythm. I see you in every group that finds its breath, every team that transcends, every moment when humans stop forcing and start flowing.

With love and endless gratitude,

Matthew

Us

Your body remembers what we forgot.

PART I: GATHER

Finding the Rhythm You Already Feel

Y our body knows something is wrong.

That tight chest during family dinners. The exhaustion no sleep can cure. The desperate need to escape from people you love. The hollow ache when groups never connect.

The three chapters that follow reveal what your body has been trying to tell you. You're not broken. You're not weak. You're recognizing rhythm violations in every group you're part of.

First, we'll name the fundamental problem—groups have forgotten they're human, treating ourselves as machines that should run continuously. Next, we'll explore how spaces participate in these rhythms. Then we'll dive into exhaustion itself as accurate data, not personal failure.

These chapters give you language for what you've been feeling. Recognition is where everything begins.

One

When Groups Forget They're Human

Y ou already know this feeling, though you might not have words for it.

It's the exhaustion that sleep doesn't cure. The tension that settles in your shoulders during family dinners that should bring joy. The hollow ache after friend gatherings that somehow leave you lonelier than before. The quiet dread that rises before volunteer meetings for causes you still believe in.

Human groups of every kind—families unfolding and refolding, friendships ebbing and flowing, communities gathering and scattering, workplaces churning through their days—I've witnessed something consistent. We've forgotten that groups are made of humans.

Not metaphorically. Actually.

Look at the evidence. Burnout spreads like wildfire—statistics confirm this across every industry—and we call it "just how things are." When someone escapes to cry in a bathroom stall at work, at church, after book club, we praise them for "handling it professionally." This perpetual connection—family group chats that never sleep, volunteer committees that never rest, work emails that never cease—has become our proof of "dedication." Exhaustion itself has transformed into a strange badge of honor, evidence of our "success."

When did this happen? When did constant depletion become the rhythm we accept?

Watch how we arrange ourselves. Families orchestrate their days like factories—every minute optimized, every child's activity stacked and scheduled for maximum efficiency. Friendships become projects to manage, with recurring calendar invites and accountability metrics. Communities measure themselves by productivity, volunteer hours tallied, outcomes quantified. Even our spiritual spaces pulse with continuous programs, endless committees, perpetual campaigns for growth.

The eight-year-old with three hours of structured activities after school, no time to watch clouds drift. The friend group that gathers every week without fail, guilt crushing anyone who needs to breathe alone. The neighborhood association with seventeen subcommittees, everyone drowning in coordination. The church that fills seven days a week with programs, burning out the very volunteers who came seeking peace.

After years documenting these patterns, one truth emerges again and again. Every exhausted group has forgotten the same essential thing.

Groups aren't machines. They're living, breathing constellations of human beings who pulse with life.

Your body has always known this. It's been singing this truth through every signal it sends. That tightness in your chest during mandatory fun? That's not anxiety—it's your body recognizing the violence of forced gathering. The flatness that settles over groups that never rest? Your body knows that humans need valleys as much as peaks. The overwhelming sensation when nothing ever completes? Your body recognizing that life itself requires endings to make space for beginnings.

Yet we keep treating ourselves like engines meant to run without pause. No downtime. No dispersal. No rest. No ending.

What Humans Actually Need

Place your hand on your chest. Feel your heartbeat—how it rises and falls, never holding peak intensity. Now notice your breathing—gathering air, then releasing, in waves that never cease yet never force. These aren't inefficiencies to optimize. They're the fundamental rhythms that keep you alive.

Human groups need the same rhythms your body does. Not metaphorically. Literally.

We're not machines that run at constant speed. We're living systems that breathe—requiring both the gathering and the dispersing. We're organisms with natural energy cycles—needing intensity to rise and fall like waves. We're ecological processes—demanding both creation and gentle decomposition.

Your nervous system already knows this. It's why your body rebels against the perpetual connectivity, why your shoulders climb toward your ears in groups that won't let you leave, why your energy flatlines in organizations that deny the natural cycles of rise and fall.

Think about how machines work—constant operation, maximum efficiency, no variation in rhythm. Downtime equals failure. Rest equals waste. Solitude equals disconnection. Endings equal loss.

Now feel how humans actually work—we gather energy like morning light, then need to release it into dusk. We come together like waves meeting shore, then need to pull back to sea. We build intensity like storms gathering, then require the quiet that follows. We create new patterns while old ones dissolve, making space for what wants to emerge.

The machine logic we've swallowed whole violates every biological rhythm. No wonder exhaustion has become our constant companion. We're forcing living systems to perform like equipment.

Your body has been keeping score. Every time you push through exhaustion instead of honoring its wisdom. Every time you stay connected when your cells cry for solitude. Every time you maintain intensity when your bones beg for rest. Every time you keep adding when your whole being needs to release.

The exhaustion isn't weakness. It's wisdom. Your body knows something your mind has been trained to ignore: Human groups can't survive without human rhythms.

I learned this the hard way.

The Team That Taught Me Everything

Twenty years ago, I coached a U14 girls soccer team that changed how I understand human groups forever.

With that team, something magical happened—though I didn't have language for it then. We found our rhythm without trying. Practice felt like breathing. The girls would arrive scattered from their different schools, carrying different days in their bodies, vibrating at different frequencies. But within minutes, we'd sync. Not through force or structure, but through something more natural, like individual streams finding their way to the same river.

We worked hard—incredibly hard. But the work had rhythm. Intense drills flowed into genuine rest. We'd gather for tactical work, then disperse for individual skills. Energy would rise toward competitions like a wave building, then fall into recovery like that same wave finding shore. Every practice had a natural completion, not just a clock-determined ending.

The girls played with joy. They rested without guilt. They ended practices feeling complete, not depleted.

We weren't soft. We were fierce competitors who won. But we won because we were alive, not because we were optimized. The rhythm made us powerful. When game time came, we had energy reserves others had exhausted in endless practices. We could surge when others were forcing. We moved like water while others moved like machinery.

Connection happened without "team-building exercises." Excellence emerged without exhausting what made us powerful. We were human beings playing a human game.

Then I moved to a different team.

Armed with what I thought was a winning formula, I tried to recreate the magic. Same drills, same schedule, same speeches. But this time, I pushed harder. If two training sessions a week worked well, three would work better. If ninety-minute sessions were good, two hours would be excellent. If the girls seemed tired, they needed to develop more stamina.

I scheduled team dinners to force the bonding that had come naturally before. Created group chats for constant connection. Added fitness sessions, video reviews, mental training. No downtime, no dispersal, no rest without purpose.

We won games. We collected trophies. We looked successful.

But the girls' eyes went flat. Parents reported anxiety that crept in at night. Joy leaked out of every drill like air from a slow puncture. Several players developed chronic injuries—their bodies breaking rather than bending. The burnout was visible, palpable, undeniable.

At the time, I blamed the girls. They weren't tough enough. They lacked commitment. They didn't want it enough.

Twenty years later, after observing hundreds of groups across every context imaginable, I feel closer to understanding what actually happened: The exhaustion wasn't from soccer. It was from forgetting these were human beings, not soccer machines.

The first team naturally maintained human rhythms—we gathered and dispersed like breathing, rose and fell like heartbeats, created and released like seasons. The second team, I forced into machine rhythm—constant gathering, perpetual intensity, endless accumulation.

I've spent two decades learning to recognize the difference. Not just in sports teams but in families that suffocate or breathe, friendships that drain or nourish, communities that exhaust or energize, organizations that consume or sustain. The pattern is consistent—when groups remember they're human, they thrive. When they forget, they slowly drown in their own exhaustion.

Why does this soccer story matter if you've never coached a day in your life? Because that soccer field was just the laboratory where I first witnessed a universal pattern.

The same dynamics that made one team thrive and another suffer despite identical training? They're operating in your marriage or partnership when date nights become obligations rather than desires. They're present in your workplace when "collaboration" becomes surveillance. They're destroying your book club that used to bring joy but now feels like homework.

A sports team makes these patterns visible because the boundaries are clear—practice starts, practice ends, season begins, season completes. But also because athletic performance reveals rhythm violations immediately. You can't hide exhaustion when you need to sprint. You can't fake vitality when the game demands everything. Bodies tell the truth on playing fields in ways we've learned to disguise everywhere else.

What I learned from those two teams wasn't about soccer. It was about recognizing the difference between groups that honor human rhythm and groups that violate it. Between excellence that emerges from vitality and achievement that comes from extraction. Between connection that forms naturally when rhythm flows and the hollow performance we force when rhythm is broken.

Those girls taught me to see what I now recognize everywhere—in boardrooms where executives make decisions at 6 PM when their cognitive rhythm has crashed, in families that schedule quality time like factory shifts, in friendships maintained through guilt rather than desire, in communities that mistake busyness for connection.

The soccer field was where I learned to read the signs. Twenty years later, I see the same patterns in every human group, just harder to recognize because we've normalized exhaustion everywhere except sport. We expect athletes to need rest between games. We forget that humans need rest between gatherings.

What This Book Offers

This book offers you language for what your body already knows.

That suffocating feeling at family gatherings where no one gets time alone? That sensation has a name. The deadness that settles over friend groups that lost their spark? That follows a pattern. The overwhelm in communities drowning in endless initiatives? That's predictable and preventable.

This book reveals three fundamental rhythms every human group needs to survive—patterns I call BREATH, PULSE, and TIDE. Your body already knows them. Now you'll have words for what you feel.

BREATH: the rhythm of gathering and dispersing, like lungs filling and emptying. PULSE: the rhythm of rising and falling, like waves building and breaking. TIDE: the rhythm of creating and dissolving, like seasons turning. Every group—from your marriage to your book club, from your volunteer committee to your work team—needs all three movements to stay vital.

These patterns flow through every group you're part of—families where chronic togetherness slowly suffocates, friend groups where forced consistency kills joy, communities where endless programs prevent actual connection, workplaces where we've learned to expect exhaustion as normal.

Here's what matters most—this isn't another system to implement. It's recognition of what's already there, waiting.

Your exhaustion isn't personal failure. It's data. Accurate information about rhythm violations in the groups you're part of. That tight chest is telling you something essential. That flat feeling carries information. That overwhelm is your body's wisdom speaking a language you're about to learn.

I've watched groups transform simply by recognizing stuck patterns. Not through complex interventions or culture initiatives. But through seeing clearly: "Oh, we're stuck in permanent gathering." "We can't let energy fall." "Nothing ever ends here."

Recognition alone often restores rhythm. Your body has been trying to tell you this for years. Now you'll have words for what you feel.

How to Use This Book

Each chapter reveals the same patterns appearing across different groups, like watching the same wave break on different shores. You'll see your family's dinner dynamics reflected in your book club's energy. You'll recognize your volunteer burnout echoing in your friend group's exhaustion. The patterns repeat because human consciousness organizes similarly regardless of context.

The practices I'll share work everywhere. The five-minute dispersion that saves a suffocating family dinner also transforms an endless work meeting. The energy descent that helps overwhelmed parents works equally for burned-out volunteers. The completion ceremony that lets friendships evolve serves congregations drowning in zombie programs.

You'll recognize yourself repeatedly. Sometimes in the exhausted parent forcing family togetherness. Sometimes in the depleted friend maintaining gatherings that lost their joy. Sometimes in the volunteer wondering why serving others feels so draining. Always in the human body trying to maintain natural rhythm in groups that forgot they're alive.

You might read straight through, following the book's own rhythm—gathering stories, pausing for patterns, releasing into practice. Or you might skip to what you need most urgently. If you're drowning in exhaustion, jump to Chapter 3. If you need immediate practices, go to Chapter 7. If you want the full pattern revealed, Chapter 4 maps all three movements in detail.

Trust your body while reading. If something feels dense, skip ahead and breathe. If something feels rushed, return to an earlier story. Your body knows what pace serves you. It knows what patterns you need to recognize first.

Start Where You Need To

"I'm exhausted and nothing's working" -> Chapter 3 (your exhaustion as data) -> Chapter 6 (immediate practices) -> Chapter 4 (diagnose what's stuck)

"My family has lost its rhythm" -> Chapter 3 (family exhaustion patterns) -> Chapter 6 (family practices) -> Chapter 4 (full pattern recognition)

"I'm skeptical about 'rhythm' talk" -> Chapter 4 (concrete observable patterns) -> Chapter 3 (exhaustion as data) -> Chapter 6 (practical experiments)

"I lead a group/team" -> Chapter 2 (group patterns across contexts) -> Chapter 4 (diagnostic application) -> Chapter 6 (micro-practices)

"Just give me the practices" -> Jump to Chapter 6 (all micro-practices) -> Work backward for context as needed

"I want the full experience" -> Read straight through—the book breathes in three parts: GATHER (stories), PAUSE (patterns), RELEASE (practice)

One request as you read—notice what happens in your body as you recognize these patterns. That moment when your shoulders finally drop because someone named what you've been feeling. The relief that washes through when you realize it's not just you. The hope that stirs when you see stuck patterns can actually shift.

Your body is the most sophisticated rhythm detector you have. It's been tracking these patterns your entire life, storing the data in your bones, your breath, your beating heart. Now you're learning to trust what it knows.

Take one deep breath before you continue. All the way in. Hold for a moment. Now release completely. Feel your chest expand and contract. That breath—that's the first rhythm. Notice how your body already knows how to gather air and release it. How it does this without your management, without optimization, without force.

Your groups need this same rhythm. They've just forgotten.

Tomorrow, you'll start noticing the held breath everywhere—in meetings that won't end, in gatherings that won't disperse, in groups that forgot they're human.

In your family dinners. In your friend group. In your volunteer work. In every human gathering you're part of.

That recognition is where everything begins. Not with fixing or forcing. Not with more trying or pushing. But with seeing clearly: Your groups have forgotten they're human. Your body hasn't.

Now you have words for what you feel.

Two

The Spaces We Share

You've felt it—how some spaces help you breathe while others slowly suffocate you. Not metaphorically. Actually. Some spaces enable natural rhythm, like lungs that know how to expand. Others architecturally prevent it, like rooms that forgot they hold humans. Your body already knows this difference in its bones.

You know the coffee shop. Not the chain on every corner with its calculated comfort, but that one specific place where regulars linger for hours, where strangers slowly become familiar, where something indefinable makes you want to stay, to settle, to breathe.

The Lighthouse Café doesn't look special. Mismatched chairs that have held countless conversations, worn tables marked by years of morning coffees, lighting that shifts with the day's moods. Watch the patterns unfold. Morning regulars at the bar, quick energy exchanged like currency. Mid-morning studiers tucked into corners, sustained focus pooling in quiet eddies. Afternoon chatters claiming center tables, social energy rising like warm air. Evening readers by windows, energy settling with the dying light.

The space holds zones for different movements—gathering at communal tables where stories merge, dispersing to corner nooks where solitude lives. High energy pulses near the espresso machine's constant dance, low energy pools by the bookshelves' quiet wisdom. New conversations spark by the door where possibility enters, old patterns maintain themselves by the fireplace where comfort lives.

Compare this to the franchise across the street. Uniform lighting that never changes, consistent seating that never surprises, regulated temperature that never varies. Every spot carries the same energy, the same expectation, the same rhythm. No corners for dispersing, no natural gathering points, no variation in the pulse. People get coffee and leave. The space has no breath, no heartbeat, no life.

The difference isn't aesthetics or coffee quality. It's rhythm architecture. One space enables all three movements—gathering and dispersing like breathing, rising and falling like heartbeats, creating new connections while letting old ones gently dissolve. The other forces single-note consistency, a monotone that exhausts through its very sameness.

Your body knows the difference immediately, before your mind can name it.

Same People, Different Rhythm

Same congregation, same people, completely different dynamics depending on the room that holds them.

Sunday services in the main sanctuary: people arrive scattered like leaves, gradually synchronize like birds finding formation, discover collective rhythm, leave unified but not depleted. The space itself guides this dance—high ceilings that allow energy to rise toward heaven, architectural focus that creates natural gathering without forcing, side chapels that enable dispersing when the soul needs quiet.

Same congregation Tuesday night in the basement conference room: fluorescent lights that buzz with mechanical insistence, drop ceiling that presses down like worry, no windows to remind bodies of the world beyond. Energy can't rise—the ceiling too low, too close, too containing. Can't disperse—the room too small, too tight, too watched. Can't find rhythm—the space has none to offer, only efficiency's empty promise.

"We've tried everything to make committee meetings work down there," Rev. Patricia told me, exhaustion threading through her voice. "Different configurations, better lighting, even prayer. Nothing helps."

The sanctuary had been shaped by 150 years of congregations, each leaving their breath in the walls. Its architecture had learned to enable natural rhythm—high ceilings that gather voices in song and let them soar, alcoves that create pools of silence for contemplation, wide doors that release people back to the world like a gentle exhale. The basement, added in 1973 for "efficient meeting space," had never developed these properties. It was built for function, not for humans.

After three years of failed meetings that felt like drowning in fluorescent light, they moved committees to the sanctuary's side chapel. Same people, same agenda, completely different outcome. The space knew how to breathe, and so the meetings found their rhythm. Decisions that had been forced for years emerged naturally, like fruit that finally ripens.

"We thought we were bad at governance," one member reflected, wonder in their voice. "Turns out we were in a room that couldn't hold human rhythm."

Connection to the Three Movements

Every group you're part of moves through three fundamental rhythms mentioned in the last chapter (we will explore them fulling in Chapter 4). Spaces either enable or restrict each of them:

BREATH (Gathering-Dispersing): Open offices force chronic gathering—no doors to close, no corners to hide, no solitude possible anywhere. The space architecturally prevents dispersing, like lungs that can only inhale. No wonder everyone's exhausted, drowning in forced proximity. But watch spaces that breathe: Old libraries with reading nooks tucked away AND community tables spread wide. Parks with gathering spaces that invite AND hidden benches that protect. They enable the full movement, the complete breath.

PULSE (Rising-Falling): Casinos design against energy falling—no windows to mark time's passage, no clocks to suggest departure, constant stimulation that never allows descent. The space architecturally prevents the falling that bodies need. People rebel but can't find the rhythm to leave, trapped in perpetual rise. Schools often make the opposite mistake—forcing constant energy suppression. Low ceilings that press down, fluorescent lights that flatten, no movement space for bodies that need to move. Energy can't rise naturally, so it erupts inappropriately, like water finding cracks.

TIDE (Creating-Dissolving): Museums architecturally prevent dissolution—everything preserved in amber, nothing allowed to complete its cycle. The space holds endless accumulation without release. Visitors often report exhaustion despite minimal physical activity, their bodies recognizing the violation. But the best community centers breathe with both permanence and change—permanent structures for essential functions AND changeable spaces for evolving needs. Some walls fixed like bones, others moveable like breath. The space enables both creation and dissolution, both forming and releasing.

The exhaustion you feel in certain spaces isn't imagination. It's your body recognizing architectural rhythm violation. Open offices that force chronic gathering like a held breath. Schools that suppress natural energy variation like a dampened flame. Hospitals that run 24/7, refusing rest even as they tend to bodies that desperately need it. We've designed spaces to enforce machine rhythms on human bodies.

Spaces that force one movement while preventing its complement will exhaust any group—family, friends, team, community. Your body has been trying to tell you this for years, in the language of tension and exhaustion, tightness and depletion.

Notice What Your Body Knows

This week, try the Threshold Pause. Before entering any space—home, office, store, friend's house—pause at the doorway for three seconds. Just three breaths at the edge of entering.

- First second: Notice what your body does. Does it lean forward with anticipation or pull back with resistance?

- Second second: Feel the space's quality washing over you. Is it pulling you toward gathering or inviting dispersal? Does it pulse with high energy or pool with quietness?

- Third second: Consciously choose to match the space's rhythm or maintain your own.

Don't analyze. Just notice:

Which spaces make your shoulders drop like setting down a weight

Which spaces make your chest tighten like a fist closing

Which spaces you avoid without thinking, your body steering you away

Which spaces you seek when you need restoration, like a plant turning toward light

After a week, you'll understand why certain buildings exhaust you and others restore you. The diagnosis takes seconds. Your body reads architectural rhythm instantly, fluently, accurately.

More importantly, you'll stop blaming yourself for exhaustion in spaces that architecturally prevent human rhythm. The exhaustion isn't your weakness or your failure to adapt.

The exhaustion isn't you. It's the space violating rhythm. Your body has been trying to tell you this for years.

Tomorrow, enter your most familiar space—home, office, café—and pause at the threshold. Three seconds. Feel what your body knows. That reaction is data about the space's rhythm. Trust it.

Three

The Exhaustion We All Feel

E veryone's exhausted. Everyone thinks it's their fault.

Not enough self-care. Poor boundaries. Wrong job. Wrong life. Need more yoga, more sleep, more vitamins, more something.

Stop. Feel your exhaustion right now. Not metaphorically—actually feel it. Where does it live in your body? That weight in your shoulders? The ache in your chest? The fog behind your eyes?

Now consider what if that exhaustion isn't yours alone? What if it's something larger, signaling through you? The rhythm violations perfected in modern workplaces—where machine logic reaches its most extreme expression—spread through exhausted bodies into every gathering we touch, like a virus of forgetting.

The exhaustion epidemic isn't about personal weakness. It's about rhythm violation at scale.

Your body has been trying to tell you this. That tight chest isn't just stress—it's your body recognizing forced gathering, the violence of never being alone. That flat feeling isn't depression—it's your body sensing stuck energy, life force with nowhere to flow. That overwhelm isn't inadequacy—it's your body drowning in accumulation without release, like lungs that can only inhale.

The exhaustion is data. Accurate information about broken patterns in the groups you're part of.

The Exhausted Parent

Jason works full-time from home. Even though his kids are back in school, he's still the default parent for sick days, early dismissals, school breaks—which means perpetual gathering mode. From the 6 AM wake-up to the 11 PM collapse, he's always visible, always available, always "on."

Morning means gathering with family for breakfast while work emails buzz beneath the table. Day means being gathered on video calls while kids interrupt for help, each interruption a small erosion. Afternoon means gathering kids for activities while work texts pierce through. Evening brings family dinner while his mind races through tomorrow's obligations. Night becomes collapsing in bed, already dreading the alarm's promise of another day exactly like this one.

"I haven't been alone in two years," he told me, voice hollow. "Actually alone. Not even in the bathroom."

Yesterday he locked himself in his car in the driveway. Just sat there for ten minutes, engine off, staring at nothing, breathing air that belonged only to him. When his ten-year-old knocked on the window—"Dad, what are you doing?"—he felt something break inside. Not dramatically. Just a quiet surrender to the impossibility of solitude.

His body shows the symptoms. Chest so tight he went to the ER thinking heart attack—it was his body trying to create space by forcing a medical emergency. Shoulders permanently raised, braced against the next invasion of his space. Breath so shallow his Apple Watch keeps reminding him to breathe, as if he's forgotten how.

The physical symptoms are just the beginning. But here's what makes it worse—Jason's energy can never actually fall. Modern parenting demands constant rising—engaged, enthusiastic, enriching. Every moment should be a teaching opportunity. Every interaction should build character. Every meal should be nutritious and mindful.

"I perform energy I don't have," he says. "Then I hate myself for being exhausted."

Jason can't create empty Saturdays—he's a single parent working two jobs. He can't take fifteen-minute solo walks—there's no one to watch the kids. He can't "just set boundaries"—his economic survival depends on being always available to his remote employer.

His exhaustion isn't personal failure. It's what happens when a human body experiences chronic gathering, forced rising, and nothing ever completing. His body is keeping accurate score of structural impossibility.

The Depleted Volunteer

Marcus volunteered for the climate action group because he cared about the future. Three years later, he's counting days until he can quit without guilt.

Every issue burns urgent. Every meeting pulses critical. Every action becomes "the most important thing we'll do." The group operates in permanent emergency—which might make sense given climate reality, except human bodies can't sustain permanent emergency without breaking.

Last month at the rally, something shifted. Marcus was holding his sign, chanting with the crowd, when suddenly he was floating above himself, watching his body go through motions. Not dramatically—just a quiet disconnection, like unplugging from his own life.

"I feel like I'm watching myself from outside," he describes, wonder and horror mixing in his voice. "Going through motions but not feeling anything."

His apartment mirrors the crisis mode—papers everywhere like fallen leaves, half-finished projects covering every surface, nothing ever reaching completion. He starts campaigns in his sleep, wakes up strategizing, falls asleep to climate anxiety. There's no valley, no rest, no integration time.

The climate group also can't complete anything. Every campaign bleeds into the next. Victories aren't celebrated because there's always another crisis. Defeats aren't processed because there's no time for grief. Nothing ends, so nothing can begin fresh.

"We had a huge victory—stopped a pipeline," Marcus says. "We celebrated for maybe five minutes. Then immediately started three new campaigns."

His nervous system never gets the satisfaction of completion. The dopamine of finishing. The rest that follows achievement. Just endless creating without dissolving, like a garden where nothing's ever harvested.

The guilt keeps him trapped. How can he prioritize his exhaustion when the planet is dying? How can he need rest when everything is urgent? The group's emotional climate makes leaving feel like betrayal—not just of the cause but of the relationships forged in crisis.

Marcus came to serve. Now he fantasizes about disappearing. Not because he stopped caring about climate—because his body can't sustain the rhythm violation. It's accurate information about unsustainable activism, but he reads it as personal weakness.

The Drained Friendship

The Thursday book club started during Evelyn's divorce. These five women saved her—showing up weekly with legally purchased substances known to help relaxation, wisdom and witness to her pain. The consistency was medicine then.

That was four years ago. Now the weekly meetings feel like prison.

"I love them," Evelyn emphasizes, as if saying it enough might make it feel true again. "But I dread Thursdays."

Starting Tuesday night, her body begins its anticipation—shoulders tightening like a spring winding, sleep fracturing into pieces. Wednesday she practices her "everything's fine" smile in the bathroom mirror, rehearsing joy she doesn't feel. Thursday afternoon she sits in her car for ten minutes before driving to book club, gathering false enthusiasm like armor.

The group can't disperse. Missing a meeting triggers group texts of concern that feel like gentle accusations. "Are you okay?" "We missed you!" "It wasn't the same without you!" The guilt crushes like slow pressure. So everyone shows up, exhausted, performing connection they no longer feel.

They also can't let energy fall. Someone's always in crisis, so energy must stay high. Someone's always celebrating, so enthusiasm is mandatory. The emotional labor of matching whatever energy the group needs has become unbearable.

"Last week, my cat died that morning," Keiko shares. "But it was Melissa's birthday celebration. So I went and pretended to be happy for three hours."

The origin story prevents honesty. How can Evelyn say she needs space from the women who saved her during divorce? The narrative of "these women are everything" makes any dispersing feel like betrayal.

The group that once gave life now drains it. Not because the friendships died—because the rhythm did. They're stuck in chronic gathering with forced energy rise. No one can say, "I need space" without seeming to reject the friendship itself.

Evelyn fantasizes about moving to another city just to have an excuse to leave the book club. The exhaustion isn't about the friendships—it's about the rhythm violation. But she has no language for this, so she thinks she's a bad friend.

The Overscheduled Child

Ten-year-old Levi's schedule:

Monday: Soccer practice 3:30-5, piano lessons 5:30-6:30, tutoring 7-8

Tuesday: Swimming 3:30-5, chess club 5:30-6:30, homework until 9

Wednesday: Soccer game 4-7, youth group 7:30-8:30

Thursday: Swimming 3:30-5, art class 5:30-7, reading program 7-8

Friday: Soccer practice 3:30-5, "family game night" (mandatory fun) 6-9

Saturday: Soccer tournament 8AM-2PM, birthday parties, playdates

Sunday: Church 9-11, family visits 12-3, prep for week 4-8

"We want to give him opportunities," his parents explain, as if opportunities were oxygen.

Levi's body tells a different story. Daily stomachaches that bloom during breakfast. Explosive rage over tiny frustrations—a broken pencil triggers twenty-three-minute meltdowns. Trouble sleeping—lies awake mentally rehearsing tomorrow's schedule like studying for a test he'll never pass.

The school counselor suggested anxiety medication.

Levi is anxious. Genuinely, measurably anxious. But his anxiety isn't emerging from nowhere—it's his nervous system responding accurately to structural impossibility. You can't eliminate falling from a child's life and expect their body not to rebel.

His energy can never fall—always performing, always achieving, always "on." His days never complete—one activity bleeds into the next without transition or breath. He never disperses—always surrounded by peers, coaches, instructors, family.

"When do you do nothing?" I asked him.

Long pause. Then, quietly: "What's nothing?"

He literally doesn't know what unstructured time feels like. His body has never experienced natural rhythm—the rise and fall of child energy like tides, the creative boredom that sparks imagination, the solitude where identity forms.

Modern childhood has become forced gathering with chronic rising and endless creating. No dispersing to discover who you are alone. No falling to integrate what you've learned. No dissolving to make space for growth.

Levi's generation is the most anxious in history. We call it a mental health crisis. I call it rhythm violation from birth.

The Elder Care Exhaustion

Adanna, sixty-two, caring for her mother with dementia. Her mother's rhythm is dissolving—memories, abilities, connections all gently releasing like leaves in autumn. But the care system forces gathering—day programs, group activities, constant stimulation.

"They keep trying to activate her," Adanna explains, exhaustion threading through every word. "But she wants to withdraw. It exhausts both of us."

Every morning, Adanna drives her mother to adult day care where cheerful staff enforce participation. Craft time when her mother wants to stare out windows. Sing-alongs when she needs silence. Exercise class when her body wants stillness. The constant activation against natural dissolution creates agitation, confusion, resistance.

Adanna's own rhythm needs dispersing—time alone to process grief, space to maintain her identity beyond caregiver. But elder care demands chronic gathering. She can't leave her mother alone. Respite care costs $30 per hour. Family helps but adds more gathering—everyone worried, everyone visiting, everyone needing updates.

The two rhythms fight constantly.

Mother needs dissolving, system demands creating. Adanna needs dispersing, situation demands gathering. Mother's energy naturally falling, activities forcing rising.

Adanna's life needs maintaining, caregiving demands everything dissolve into this one role.

"We're both drowning," Adanna says. "She's drowning in too much stimulation. I'm drowning in no space to breathe."

Last week, exhausted, Adanna let her mother skip day care. They sat in the garden all morning, not talking, barely moving, breathing together in silence. Her mother's agitation disappeared like mist. Adanna felt her chest unknot for the first time in months. But the next day, back to the program—Medicare only pays if her mother attends regularly.

The exhaustion isn't from caregiving itself but from forcing opposite rhythms. Making someone whose tide is going out pretend the tide is coming in. Making someone who needs solitude perform constant togetherness. Both bodies keeping accurate score of this rhythm warfare.

Your Body as Rhythm Detector

Certain signals appear frequently when rhythms stick. But here's what matters most: your body is the authority on what it's telling you, not these observations.

What I'm offering below are common patterns I've observed—patterns that might help you recognize what you're feeling. But if your tight chest means something completely different than what I describe, trust that. If your exhaustion speaks a different language, listen to it. These patterns are starting points for your own noticing, not definitions of what you should be experiencing.

Your body's wisdom is more sophisticated than any pattern I can map.

What Your Chest Tells You

Tight chest, can't get full breath: You're stuck in chronic gathering. Your body is trying to create space by limiting breath. It's saying, "We can't take in anymore—we need to release."

Hollow chest, empty feeling: You're stuck in chronic dispersing. Your body is signaling disconnection. It's saying, "We need real gathering—not performed proximity but actual connection."

What Your Energy Tells You

Wired but tired: You're stuck in chronic rising. Your body is forcing energy that isn't there. Adrenaline and cortisol maintaining artificial elevation. You're running on stress hormones, not vitality.

Flat, numb, absent: You're stuck in chronic falling or forced falling. Your body has given up trying to rise. Or it's protecting you from unsustainable intensity by disconnecting.

What Your Mind Tells You

Overwhelmed, can't prioritize: You're stuck in chronic creating. Too much has accumulated. Your executive function is drowning in undissolved obligations.

Scattered, can't focus: You're stuck in chronic dissolving. Nothing stable to organize around. Your mind needs something solid to orient toward.

The Compound Effect

Most exhaustion isn't from single rhythm violation. It's from multiple violations compounding:

Jason the parent: Chronic gathering + forced rising + no dissolution = total system breakdown pending

Marcus the volunteer: Chronic rising + no completion + forced gathering = dissociation

Evelyn's book club: Chronic gathering + forced energy matching + no dissolution = relationship exhaustion

Levi the child: Chronic activation + no dispersing + no dissolution = childhood anxiety epidemic

Adanna the caregiver: Opposing rhythms + chronic gathering + forced rising = mutual destruction

Your exhaustion is probably multiple violations stacking. That's why single interventions fail. "Self-care" can't fix chronic gathering. "Boundaries" can't fix forced rising. "Mindfulness" can't fix lack of dissolution.

The Scale of Violation

The violations aren't just personal. They're operating at every scale simultaneously.

Cultural Level:

- 24/7 economy (no collective falling)

- Social media (chronic gathering)

- Productivity culture (chronic rising)

- Consumer accumulation (no dissolution)

Institutional Level:

- Schools enforce chronic activation with no rest periods

- Healthcare prioritizes efficiency over rhythm

- Workplaces impose machine schedules on human bodies

- Cities eliminate quiet, dark, and solitude

Community Level:

- Over-programmed churches, temples, and centers

- Volunteer organizations locked in permanent crisis

- Neighborhoods with no dispersing spaces

- Social groups that can't say no

Family Level:

- No empty time on calendars

- Forced family togetherness

- Children treated as productivity projects

- Elders forced into activation

Individual Level:

- Bodies that forgot how to fall

- Minds that can't stop creating

- Hearts that can't release

- Spirits that can't find rhythm

In the contexts I can observe—post-industrial, digitally-connected populations—rhythm violation is systematic. But these violations aren't equally distributed. Those with less power—economically marginalized, structurally oppressed, lacking safety or agency—often bear the greatest rhythm violations.

A CEO who institutes "valley weeks" has different capacity than a contract cleaner experiencing the same chronic rising. Both feel the exhaustion, but only one can change the schedule. This structural reality shapes everything about rhythm restoration.

The exhaustion is accurate data about what we've built—a world that violates human rhythm at every scale.

Recognition as Beginning

You can't fix all of this. The violations are structural, systematic, beyond individual solution.

But you can recognize it. And recognition changes everything.

When Jason names "I'm stuck in chronic gathering," he stops blaming himself for exhaustion. He might find twenty minutes to sit in his car. Not enough, but something.

When Marcus recognizes "This group only knows rising," he can choose when to match that rhythm and when to honor his own fall. He might stay involved but protect his energy.

When Evelyn admits "This friendship pattern exhausts me," she can have an honest conversation. The group might find new rhythm or might dissolve. Either is better than forced performance.

When Levi's parents see "We've eliminated falling from his life," they might cancel one activity. Just one. His body might remember what descent feels like.

When Adanna understands "We're in opposite rhythms," she stops forcing her mother to activate. She might find moments of parallel rhythm—both resting even if not together.

Recognition doesn't solve the problem. But it relocates the problem from personal failure to pattern violation. From "what's wrong with me" to "what rhythm is being broken."

That shift is everything.

Stand up right now. Shake your whole body for five seconds. Just shake everything loose. Feel that release? Notice how your body knows exactly how to let go? It's been trying to do that for years. The exhaustion is data about what's preventing that release.

Tomorrow you'll notice rhythm violations everywhere—in your morning routine, your commute, your meetings, your family dinner. Don't fight them all. Just recognize them. That recognition is the first breath of a different rhythm. And once you can name what's stuck, you'll start seeing the three movements that every group needs to stay alive.

PART II: PAUSE

The Pattern Between Breaths

Now we slow down to see what's actually happening.

You've recognized the exhaustion. You've felt how spaces shape rhythm. You understand that your tiredness means something deeper. Like the pause between inhaling and exhaling, this middle section creates space to understand the patterns beneath.

Chapter 4 maps the three fundamental movements every human group needs to stay alive. Through examples at every scale—families, friendships, communities, workplaces—you'll see the same patterns repeating everywhere. BREATH (gathering-dispersing). PULSE (rising-falling). TIDE (creating-dissolving). By the chapter's end, these movements will be undeniable.

Chapter 5 reveals how these movements interact, sometimes creating perfect flow, sometimes generating crushing exhaustion. You'll understand why certain times consistently create conflict and why others flow effortlessly.

This pause prepares you for practice. You can't restore rhythm until you recognize what rhythm is and how it wants to move.

Four

How Groups Stay Alive

E very group you're part of—family dinners that should nourish but deplete, friend gatherings that should connect but isolate, volunteer work that should inspire but exhaust, team meetings that should create but stagnate—moves through three fundamental rhythms. When these rhythms flow, groups feel alive. When they get stuck, everyone drowns in exhaustion.

The same three movements appear everywhere. Not metaphorically. Literally.

These patterns appear in every human group. But nowhere are they more visible—more extreme, more systematic, more measurable—than in modern workplaces. Organizations have perfected the art of forgetting humans need rhythm. They become laboratories where violations are refined, then exported through tired bodies to every other part of life.

If you want to see chronic gathering in its purest form, look at the open office where privacy died. If you want to see chronic rising perfected, watch sprint culture consume itself. If you want to see endless accumulation, count the zombie projects that no one dares to end.

The same patterns suffocate families, drain friendships, and exhaust communities. But workplaces make them undeniable.

These aren't frameworks to implement. They're patterns already present in every human gathering, waiting to be recognized, like constellations that were always there before we learned to see them.

BREATH: Gathering-Dispersing

Ever notice how some gatherings feel suffocating even when you love the people?

That desperate need to step outside during family holidays, as if the walls themselves are closing in. The bathroom break that's really an escape from the book club, five minutes of blessed solitude. The overwhelming urge to be alone after volunteer meetings, even though you believe in the cause with your whole heart.

Then there's the opposite—that hollow feeling when a group never really comes together. Remote teams where everyone's present but no one's connected, pixels on screens pretending to be people. Families living like ships passing in the night, sharing a house but not a life.

Observing human groups, here's what I consistently see. Groups need to breathe. They need to come together fully, then separate completely. Gather and disperse. Inhale and exhale. Like lungs that know both filling and emptying are essential.

This isn't about introversion or extroversion. It's about fundamental human rhythm. Watch any healthy group and you'll see it—the natural pulse of connection and solitude, like a heart that knows both contraction and release.

Family

The Okonkwo-Johnsons did everything together. Grocery shopping, errands, meals, evenings, weekends—all of it shared, always. They called it "family time" and wore it like a badge of honor.

"We're so close," they'd tell anyone who'd listen, as if proximity equaled intimacy.

But their bodies told a different story. Ade's shoulders stayed raised, braced against an invasion that never stopped. David sat in his car for ten minutes before coming inside each day, stealing moments of solitude like a thief. Their teenage daughter Kimi lingered late at school—just sitting in the library, breathing air that belonged to no one else. The eight-year-old, Kai, began having daily meltdowns that shook the house.

Then Ade read about "family breathing room" and tried an experiment. Twenty minutes every evening, everyone disperses. No explanation, no activities, just twenty minutes alone. David walks around the block, letting his thoughts unspool. Ade sits in the bedroom with the door closed, feeling her edges return. Kimi retreats to their room, existing without performance. Kai plays in the backyard alone, discovering who they are without witnesses.

The first week felt wrong, like a betrayal of everything they'd built. "Are we falling apart?" Ade worried, watching her family scatter.

Week two, something shifted. They came back together for dinner differently—hungrier for each other's presence.

Stories bubbled up that hadn't been shared in months, emerging from the space silence had created.

By month two, Kai's tantrums stopped. Completely. As if the pressure valve had finally been opened.

"We didn't need less love," Ade told me later, wonder in her voice. "We needed to breathe."

Friends

The Wednesday Walking Group had been meeting weekly for eight years. Same six women, same park trail, same 7 AM start time, reliable as sunrise.

It started during Yasmin's divorce when movement felt like the only thing keeping her from dissolving completely. These women became her anchor, her witnesses, her survival.

But that was eight years ago. Now the weekly meetings felt like prison. The group text planning each week grew tense with unspoken resentments. "Can't make it" triggered guilt spirals that lasted days. They'd show up, bodies present, going through motions of connection, but something vital had died.

Yasmin finally said what everyone felt: "I love you all, but I'm drowning in obligation."

The silence that followed wasn't shock. It was relief, like a held breath finally released.

They instituted monthly meetings with a "no-show" option—once a month, anyone could skip without explanation. No guilt allowed. No questions asked.

First monthly meeting brought four out of six women. The two who didn't send heart emojis—no explanations, no apologies, just love without obligation. The four who gathered walked for two hours instead of one. Real stories emerged from the space between them. Deep laughter returned, surprising them all.

"We thought friendship meant never letting go," Yasmin told me. "Turns out it means knowing when to hold tight and when to release."

Community

The Riverside Neighborhood Association started with forty families excited about creating connection. Monthly meetings became committees, then subcommittees, then a WhatsApp group requiring daily check-ins, like a spreading web that trapped instead of supported.

Within two years, active participation had dropped to six families—burnt out but unable to stop, caught in the momentum of their own creation.

The president, Mx. Jamie Chen, felt like they were "breathing for the entire neighborhood." A broken streetlight triggered three committee meetings. A proposed stop sign generated fifty-seven group messages. Every small decision became an exhausting production.

The breaking point came during a Tuesday night "emergency meeting" about holiday decorations. Three people showed up. Jamie looked at the empty chairs and started crying—not dramatic sobs, just quiet tears of recognition. "We're killing this community with togetherness."

They dissolved everything except quarterly meetings. No committees. No group chat. Just four gatherings a year, optional attendance.

The first quarterly meeting brought twelve families—double the recent average. Six months later, thirty families attended the spring gathering. Without forced gathering, people actually wanted to gather. Desire replaced obligation.

Workplace

TechFlow's open office was designed for "maximum collaboration." No walls, no doors, no privacy anywhere. Every desk visible from every other desk, like a panopticon of productivity.

The architecture enforced chronic gathering. Always visible. Always available. Always together. Always performing connection.

Productivity dropped despite longer hours. People came in at 6 AM or stayed until 9 PM—not to work more, but to experience the office empty, to remember what solitude felt like. The parking lot became a refuge where employees ate lunch in their cars, windows cracked for air that wasn't shared.

The breaking point came when their best developer quit with one sentence: "I haven't been alone in two years."

The CEO instituted "Deep Work Wednesdays"—no meetings, no collaboration, no interaction. The resistance was fierce. "We'll lose our culture!" they cried, as if culture meant surveillance.

But bodies started relaxing, shoulders dropping for the first time in months. And something unexpected happened—the other four days became more collaborative, not less. People chose to gather because they'd been allowed to disperse.

"We thought open office meant open collaboration," the CEO told me. "We didn't realize we were suffocating our humanity."

Culture

Look at modern life—chronic gathering at every scale. Social media ensures we're never alone, notifications pulling us back whenever we drift toward solitude. Cities dense beyond comprehension, humans stacked like items in storage. Homes designed without private spaces because "open concept brings families together," as if together was the only direction that mattered.

Some communities once held more rhythm between gathering and dispersing. Sunday gathering for worship, then dispersing to separate spaces. Seasonal rhythms that honored both connection and solitude. Though this rhythm was never universal—many people's ancestors experienced forced proximity. Dispersing has always been a privilege unevenly distributed.

But whatever rhythm existed has accelerated toward chronic gathering. We celebrate constant connection and pathologize solitude. Productivity culture demands visibility. Digital platforms monetize our inability to be alone.

No wonder anxiety spreads like wildfire—we're asking billions to sustain permanent gathering with no rhythm of release.

Diagnostic Questions

Look at any group you're part of and ask:

- Can this group gather deeply?

- Can this group disperse completely?

- What does your body tell you?

Tight chest = stuck in gathering.
Hollow feeling = stuck in dispersing.
Natural breathing = rhythm is flowing.

Micro-Practice

Tomorrow, in any group you're part of, take five minutes of complete dispersal. No explanation, just five minutes alone. Step outside. Find an empty room. Sit in your car.

Notice what happens in your body when you're alone. Notice what happens when you return. Five minutes of actual dispersing can shift the entire rhythm of a stuck group.

PULSE: Rising-Falling

Ever notice groups that feel manic—always pushing, always urgent, always at maximum intensity? Or groups that feel dead—no energy, no spark, nothing alive?

The data shows the same thing everywhere. Groups need their energy to rise AND fall. Not randomly, but rhythmically. Like a heartbeat that knows both systole and diastole. Like waves that build and break. Like every living thing that pulses with life.

Energy that only rises eventually crashes, leaving wreckage. Energy that never rises eventually dies, leaving ghosts. The pulse between these movements keeps groups alive.

Family

The Preston household had been underwater for eight months.

It started when David lost his job—not just any job, but the career he'd built for fifteen years. The one that had moved them to Ithaca, bought the house, defined who he was. After that, something in the family's energy broke.

Dinner became silent, mechanical. Pass the salt. Clear the plates. No one looked up. The kids, thirteen and nine, moved through the house like ghosts, their natural child-energy suppressed by the weight in the air. Birthday parties came and went, celebrated with cake but no joy. Maria kept working, kept functioning, but a flatness had settled over everything.

"We're managing," Maria would say when friends asked. Managing meant surviving. Managing meant no one's energy could rise because rising felt like betrayal of David's pain.

Their nine-year-old, Lily, started getting in trouble at school. Not for misbehavior—for being "too quiet." Teacher notes: "Lily seems withdrawn." "Lily doesn't participate." "Is everything okay at home?"

Everything was not okay. But not in the way people thought.

Maria's sister, Rosa, visited for a weekend. She watched the silent dinners, the flat affect, the way everyone moved through emotional molasses. Sunday morning, she did something radical—she put on music. Loud, ridiculous pop music. Started dancing badly in the kitchen.

David looked up, confused. The kids stared. Maria started to object—

But Lily laughed. Actually laughed, bright and sudden like a match striking.

Rosa kept dancing, beckoned Lily over. Then the thirteen-year-old joined, embarrassed but smiling. Then Maria, tentative. David watched for a long moment, then—impossibly—stood up and shuffled his feet.

Five minutes of terrible dancing. That's all it was.

But something cracked open. At dinner that night, conversation happened. Small, halting, but real. The kids told school stories they'd been holding back for months. David mentioned an interview he had next week—first time he'd spoken about the future in months.

"I thought we had to stay in the pain together," Maria told me later. "I thought rising meant pretending everything was fine, toxic positivity. But Aunt Rosa showed us—rising isn't pretending. It's remembering we're still alive."

They instituted "Sunday music mornings." Sometimes David couldn't participate—the grief still too heavy. But the kids could dance. Maria could smile. Energy could rise in parts of the family even when not everyone was ready.

Six months later, David had a new job. But more than that—the house felt alive again. Not because the hard thing had resolved, but because they'd learned energy could fall AND rise. Grief could coexist with joy. Struggle with laughter.

"We were stuck in the valley," David reflected. "We needed permission to climb out, even if just for a few minutes at a time."

Volunteer

The Environmental Action Group had been in crisis mode for three years straight. Every issue burned urgent, every meeting thrummed intense, every action pulsed critical.

Alejandro, the lead organizer, hadn't taken a break in three years. "We don't have the luxury of rest. The planet is dying."

Then Alejandro collapsed. Literally. At a protest, body finally refusing what mind demanded. Dehydration, exhaustion, adrenal fatigue—their body simply stopped, like an engine seizing.

From the hospital bed, pale as the sheets: "Take August off."

The resistance was immediate and fierce. "We can't stop now!"

But Alejandro's collapse had scared them. They took August off.

September first, they reconvened. All twelve core volunteers returned—plus five new people who'd been watching from the sidelines, too exhausted by the visible intensity to join.

They instituted "fallow months"—August and December. No actions, no meetings, optional participation. Time for the soil to rest.

Their most successful campaign—saving the wetlands—emerged after their first fallow December. It came from a volunteer who'd spent the quiet month walking those wetlands daily, no agenda, just presence.

"We were so busy fighting we forgot that creation requires rest," someone reflected.

Community

The Riverside Interfaith Community had been in "growth mode" for seven years. More members, more programs, more services, more everything. The building blazed with light seven days a week, as if darkness was failure.

"A spiritual center that never sleeps," they proclaimed proudly.

But volunteer burnout reached epidemic levels. The same twelve people ran everything while three hundred others attended wrapped in guilt.

The youth coordinator quit with one line that haunted them: "I've forgotten how to sabbath."

A spiritual community that had forgotten rest—the very thing every tradition commanded.

They instituted "quiet seasons"—periods when contemplative practices took precedence. Ramadan became about actual reflection, not events. Advent focused on waiting, not producing.

Some people left—those addicted to constant intensity. But more people came. Exhausted people searching for permission to rest, to be still, to stop producing their worth.

The community didn't grow numerically that year. But depth grew. Relationships deepened. Joy returned like a forgotten friend.

"Rest isn't absence of devotion," Imam Hassan reflected. "Rest IS devotion."

Workplace

The tech hub operated in permanent sprint mode. Every project urgent. Every deadline yesterday. The office thrummed with manic energy from 7 AM to midnight, like a heart racing toward failure.

They burned through talent. Average tenure measured eleven months before bodies gave out.

Then three developers were hospitalized in one month. Heart palpitations. Panic disorders. One stroke at age thirty-two.

The board forced a "rest week." No meetings. No deadlines. No Slack. Mandatory nothing.

That week, employees didn't know what to do. Energy forced high for so long didn't know how to descend.

By Wednesday, something shifted. People started walking without destinations. Thinking—actually thinking, not just reacting to the next emergency.

Friday, the CTO had an insight that solved a six-month problem. It came while sitting in the park, doing absolutely nothing.

They instituted "valley weeks" after every major launch. Their next product launch was their most successful ever. Teams that could rest could innovate.

"We thought constant intensity meant we were serious," the CEO admitted. "Turns out it meant we were scared."

Culture

American culture only knows one direction—up. Growth quarters. Productivity increases. More, better, faster, always ascending.

We medicate exhaustion instead of honoring it. Caffeine to force morning energy. Alcohol to force evening descent. Sleeping pills because bodies forgot how to fall naturally.

In cultures that still honor rhythm, energy rises and falls daily, weekly, seasonally. Siestas aren't laziness—they're honoring the afternoon descent. Sabbaths aren't religious antiquity—they're survival patterns.

We've replaced natural rhythm with forced consistency. Every day the same productivity. No wonder we're exhausted.

Diagnostic Questions

- **Can energy rise naturally here?**

- **Can energy fall without shame?**

- **What does your body tell you?**

Racing heart = stuck in rise.
Heavy limbs = stuck in fall.
Natural vitality = rhythm is flowing.

Micro-Practice

This week, declare one "low tide" hour in any group. One hour where nothing is scheduled, nothing productive happens, just gentle existing together.

Notice what your body does when allowed to descend. Notice what happens to the group's energy afterwards. Notice if that valley makes the next peak possible.

TIDE: Creating-Dissolving

Ever notice how groups accumulate everything but release nothing?

Every tradition, every project, every commitment piling up year after year like sediment. The family maintaining rituals nobody enjoys. The organization with forty-seven initiatives, most walking dead.

Then there's the opposite—groups where nothing stabilizes. Constant reorganization. Everything dissolving before it can take root, like building on quicksand.

Here's what I see. Groups need to create AND dissolve. Begin AND end. Like tides that bring in and carry out, this rhythm keeps groups from drowning in their own accumulation.

Family

The Chang family honored everything. Lunar New Year celebrations and Mid-Autumn festivals. Thanksgiving and Christmas. The hybrid traditions they'd created together—Saturday dumpling making, Sunday pancake breakfasts. School traditions the kids brought home like stray cats.

The calendar looked like a battlefield. No white space anywhere.

"We're so rich in traditions," Mom would say, exhaustion bleeding through her smile.

The breaking point came during President's Day weekend—the only weekend without a tradition. Dad suggested doing something spontaneous. The family literally couldn't. Every idea got measured against existing traditions, found wanting or conflicting.

Their ten-year-old said quietly: "We can't do anything new because we're too busy doing everything old."

That night, Mom and Dad counted—forty-three separate traditions. Forty-three.

They held a tradition funeral. Each family member could release one tradition with gratitude. They lit candles, shared favorite memories, then blew them out. "Thank you for the joy you brought. We release you with love."

The space that opened was immediate. The next month had eight empty weekend days—blank spaces like promises.

New patterns emerged organically. Spontaneous hiking when the weather called. Lazy Sundays that asked nothing. A new tradition of "tradition-free months."

"We thought traditions meant love," Mom reflected. "But we'd become curators of a museum, not a living family."

Friends

The book club had met monthly for eight years. Same format since year one, crystallized in amber.

Somewhere around year six, it calcified. The format that once enabled discussion now constrained it. The connection that once felt vital now felt obligatory.

"I dread it," Courtney finally admitted. "I love you all, but I dread book club."

The silence was relieved, not shocked. Everyone had been feeling it.

They held a funeral for the old format. Brought the binders of discussion guides and recipe cards. Spent two hours celebrating what had been. Then literally buried the format in Jennifer's backyard, returning it to earth.

The next month, they met without structure. No assigned book. No requirements. Just women, wine, and whatever wanted to emerge.

It was chaotic. And alive. Truly alive for the first time in years.

"We thought the structure was holding us together," Courtney reflected. "Turns out it was holding us back."

Community

First Community Center had forty-seven official programs. Youth Chess Club (three members, all seniors). Men's Breakfast (average age seventy-eight). Programs that hadn't met in years but lived on in the budget.

The new director attended every program for two months. Seventeen never met. Twelve had fewer than three attenders.

They introduced "completion ceremonies." Once a month, any program ready to end could have formal completion. Not failure—completion.

The Youth Chess Club went first. Three elderly men set up boards one last time, played a ceremonial final move. "This club served our community for thirty years. We release it with gratitude."

Within six months, twenty-three programs had dissolved with dignity. The budget freed up $60,000.

New life emerged immediately. Young families started "Messy Art." Teenagers created climate action groups. Recent immigrants launched story circles.

"We were so busy maintaining the past, we couldn't create a future," one elder reflected.

Culture

Look at the nearly $50 billion personal storage industry. We pay to warehouse things we don't use because we can't let them go.

We accumulate everything, release nothing. Not just material—psychological, relational, organizational. We maintain friendships that died years ago. Hold grievances, traditions, structures that no longer serve.

Workplaces perfect this accumulation. The average corporation maintains 47 initiatives while serving fewer actual needs. Zombie projects consume millions. Legacy systems drain 40% of IT budgets. Every merger adds programs nobody dissolves. Organizations become graveyards of good intentions because ending feels like failure, so they accumulate until they collapse under their own weight.

Marie Kondo became global because she gave permission to release. "Thank it and let it go" became revolutionary because we'd forgotten gratitude could accompany endings.

We've forgotten that decomposition feeds new growth. That endings enable beginnings. That death makes life possible.

Diagnostic Questions

- **Can new things begin here?**

- **Can old things end with dignity?**

- **What does your body tell you?**

Overwhelmed = too much creating, not enough dissolving.

Groundless = too much dissolving, not enough creating.

Natural flow = rhythm is working.

Micro-Practice

This week, name one thing ready to complete. Could be tiny—a tradition nobody enjoys, an exhausting group text.

Name it to someone: "I think X is ready to complete."

If possible, thank it before releasing: "This served us by... We release it with gratitude."

Then actually let it end. Notice the space that opens. Notice what wants to emerge.

The Recognition

You've now seen the same three patterns at every scale. Family, friends, community, workplace, culture—same rhythms everywhere, like fractals repeating.

This isn't coincidence. It's how human consciousness organizes. Every group needs to breathe (gathering-dispersing), pulse (rising-falling), and flow like tides (creating-dissolving).

Your body has been recognizing these patterns your entire life. That suffocating feeling at family dinners? BREATH stuck. The flat exhaustion in friend groups? PULSE stuck. The overwhelm in organizations? TIDE stuck.

Tomorrow, you'll start seeing stuck patterns everywhere. More importantly, you'll have language for what you're seeing.

Recognition alone often restores rhythm. Just naming "we're stuck in chronic gathering" can create the first exhale. Identifying "we never let energy fall" can initiate the first descent.

You don't need to manage these rhythms. You need to recognize them, then get out of their way. They want to flow. They just need you to stop preventing what's already trying to happen.

Stand up. Take a deep breath while raising your arms (gathering + rising). Now exhale while lowering them (dispersing + falling). Feel something releasing (old) while something else wants to form (new). You just performed all three movements in ten seconds.

Your body knows exactly how to do this. So does every group you're part of. They've just forgotten. Now you can remind them.

Five

When Rhythms Interact

The three movements don't happen in isolation. They weave together, influence each other, create patterns within patterns like threads in a living tapestry.

The three movements don't happen in isolation. They weave together, creating patterns within patterns. BREATH enables PULSE. PULSE drives TIDE. TIDE requires BREATH. When these movements harmonize, groups flow effortlessly, like a river finding its course. When they conflict, exhaustion multiplies, compounding like interest on a debt you never agreed to carry.

Your body already knows this. You've felt the relief when all three movements align—that rare day when your family's gathering coincides with rising energy and something new beginning. You've felt the opposite too, when every rhythm fights every other rhythm, and you can't find flow anywhere, like swimming against multiple currents at once.

But here's what's crucial to understand—these aren't mechanical laws. In reality, every movement influences every other movement in ways that shift with context, scale, and moment. What I'm showing you in this chapter are specific patterns I've observed frequently enough to name.

But the movements weave together like living systems, not like machine parts. As you observe your own groups, you'll discover interactions I haven't seen, connections that contradict what I've described, movements that influence each other in ways unique to your context.

This isn't failure of the movements—it's the nature of living rhythm. We're not mapping a machine. We're recognizing a dance.

How Movements Enable Each Other

While the three movements interact in complex ways, certain patterns appear consistently. Here are the clearest connections I've observed.

Gathering Enables Rising

Watch any group that gathers well—really comes together with full presence. Energy naturally begins to rise like morning light spreading across water.

The Nguyen family discovered this accidentally. They'd been trying to force morning energy for years. Alarm clocks shrieking, rushed breakfasts, everyone scattered before actually waking up. Days felt flat before they began, like trying to start a fire with wet wood.

Then an ice storm knocked out their internet for a week. No morning scroll. No immediate dispersion into individual screens. They had to actually gather at breakfast—eye contact, conversation, presence without the digital escape routes.

By day three, something shifted. Energy started rising naturally. Not forced enthusiasm but genuine vitality. The teenager who usually grunted through breakfast started sharing dreams from the night before. The ten-year-old began planning adventures for after school. The parents found themselves laughing—actual laughter at 7 AM in the middle of winter.

"We'd been trying to manufacture energy," Lin told me. "But energy can't rise if you never actually gather."

They kept the internet off during breakfast even after power returned. That genuine gathering—fifteen minutes of actual presence—enabled the energy rise that carried them through their days.

Why does this work? Human nervous systems co-regulate. When bodies are truly present together, energy synchronizes and amplifies. Mirror neurons fire, emotional contagion spreads, collective attention creates resonance. Genuine gathering creates the conditions for natural rising.

But forced gathering—like corporate "mandatory fun"—doesn't enable rising. Bodies know the difference between gathering that enables versus gathering that suffocates.

Falling Enables Dissolving

When energy is low, letting go becomes possible.

The Shady family discovered this during COVID lockdown. Their usual energy—soccer at local fields, weekend activities scattered across the county, the constant momentum of normal life—suddenly stopped. Energy fell to levels they'd never experienced. Days became quiet, slow, almost dreamlike, like the town itself in deep winter.

In that low energy, they could finally see what needed to release.

The Saturday soccer their son had outgrown—in the low energy, he simply said, "I don't want to go back."

The monthly dinner parties they'd been hosting—in the quiet, they admitted, "We don't enjoy this anymore." The performance of entertaining, the forced cheer, the cleanup exhaustion.

The friendship that had been draining them for years—in the stillness, they could finally feel its cost.

"We'd been too busy to notice what needed to end," James told me. "The forced energy drop let us finally see what we'd been carrying."

They released seven major commitments during lockdown. When energy returned with spring's arrival, they didn't resume any of them.

High energy maintains everything—even what's dead. Low energy allows entropy. Just as molecules need low temperature to settle into new arrangements, groups need energy valleys to release old patterns. You can't let go while running.

When Rhythms Harmonize

Sometimes, miraculously, all three movements align. These are the moments when groups transcend normal functioning.

The Martinez Family Discovery

The Martinez family couldn't figure out why Thursday evenings were always disasters. Family planning meetings at 8 PM seemed logical—everyone was home, weekend approaching, perfect time to coordinate.

But every Thursday meeting ended in tears, arguments, or sullen silence.

Maria started tracking what she felt in her body each Thursday. Tight chest by 6 PM. Shoulders climbing by 7. By 8, when they were supposed to plan together, her jaw was clenched so tight she could barely speak civilly.

Then she mapped what was happening.

Thursday 8 PM was a rhythm collision. Their daily rhythm had energy naturally falling toward bedtime. Their weekly rhythm showed Thursday exhaustion from four days of work and school. The family rhythm had everyone needing to disperse after forced gathering all week. And the creating/dissolving pattern meant the week was dissolving but they were forcing themselves to create next week's structure.

They were trying to gather when bodies wanted dispersing. Trying to raise energy for planning when everything was falling. Trying to create new structure when the week was dissolving.

"We were fighting four different rhythms simultaneously," Maria realized.

They moved family meetings to Saturday morning at 10 AM. Different story entirely. Daily rhythm had energy naturally rising with morning light. Weekly rhythm showed bodies rested from Friday night's sleep. Family rhythm meant genuinely wanting to gather after Friday's dispersal. Creating/dissolving aligned with the natural time for new weekly patterns to form.

The difference was immediate. Decisions that took two painful hours Thursday night took thirty pleasant minutes Saturday morning. Same family, same agenda, completely different outcome.

"We weren't bad at planning," Maria reflected. "We were planning at the worst possible time."

Finding Your Sweet Spot

Every group has times when rhythms naturally align. The design studio discovered theirs—Friday afternoon project completions. Daily falling merged with weekly falling merged with project dissolving. Perfect release. The satisfaction was total.

Your family might find it's Sunday morning (rested + gathering + creating) or Wednesday evening (mid-week gather + energy sustained + maintaining).

The key is recognizing when multiple rhythms support the same movement versus when they fight.

When Rhythms Conflict

Most exhaustion comes not from single rhythm violations but from rhythms fighting each other. Your body caught between incompatible demands.

Thursday Evening Crisis

Sarah at 6 PM Thursday perfectly illustrates modern rhythm collision.

Her workplace demands a late meeting scheduled—forced gathering when she's been gathered all day. Critical budget decisions require forced rising when energy is naturally falling. New initiative planning means creating when the week should be dissolving.

Her family needs something different. Eight-year-old daughter anxious about tomorrow's test needs gathering for comfort. Bedtime routine requires supporting daughter's falling energy. No backup parent available.

Her volunteer commitment at the food bank adds another layer. Monthly board meeting tonight requires gathering. As treasurer, budget approval needs rising energy for complex decisions. New fundraising campaign demands creating.

Meanwhile, her body's actual state tells its own truth. Desperate need to disperse after meetings since 8 AM. Natural evening pulse falling. End of intense week means weekly tide dissolving.

Four different groups making incompatible demands on one body. Work wants gather, rise, create. Family needs gather, fall, maintain. Volunteer requires gather, rise, create. Body demands disperse, fall, dissolve.

This isn't personal failure. This is structural impossibility.

Sarah's solution was imperfect but necessary. Called into work meeting from her car in the parking lot while walking circles. Texted volunteer board she'd review materials later. Rushed home for abbreviated bedtime routine.

Everyone slightly disappointed. Sarah exhausted not from activity but from rhythm warfare.

Weekend Rhythm Wars

Jack and Priya discovered their weekend exhaustion wasn't relationship problems—it was rhythm collision.

Jack's workweek at the aerospace company meant constant client-facing, forced gathering, performing enthusiasm. By Friday, desperate for dispersing and falling.

Priya's workweek doing remote data analysis for the university meant isolation all week. By Friday, desperate for gathering and rising.

Their weekend needs were perfectly opposite. They stopped trying to share weekend rhythms. Saturday mornings, Priya goes to the park and yoga class downtown—gathering and rising. Jack stays home gardening alone—dispersing and falling. They reconvene Saturday evening when rhythms align.

"We stopped thinking togetherness meant same rhythm," Priya reflected.

Cultural Rhythm Mismatch

The Park family—Korean parents, American teenagers—lived in constant rhythm conflict.

Parents expected extended family constantly gathered, children participating in everything, individual needs subordinate to family rhythm.

Teenagers needed privacy for identity development, peer relationships, periodic dispersal from family.

The breakthrough came when they named it as rhythm conflict, not values conflict. They developed hybrid rhythm—three weeknight dinners with full gathering, two nights where teenagers could take plates to rooms.

"We thought our children were rejecting our culture," the mother reflected. "They were trying to survive in two different rhythm systems."

Quick Conflict Patterns

BREATH and PULSE conflict when morning meetings happen while half the team's energy hasn't risen yet.

PULSE and TIDE conflict during year-end fundraising push when organizational energy should be falling.

BREATH and TIDE conflict means you can't gather to complete projects, can't disperse to create new ones.

All three conflicting looks like Friday afternoon restructuring announcements—forced gathering, forced rising, forced creating when everything wants to fall and dissolve.

Workplace Conflict Extremes

Post-vacation blues mean your body's in vacation rhythm while work demands immediate production rhythm.

Merger failures happen when two incompatible rhythm systems get forced together.

Startup burnout follows chronic everything with no relief—usually crisis within 3-6 months.

These workplace conflicts don't stay at work—exhausted bodies carry these broken rhythms into every family dinner, every friendship, every community gathering.

Reading Rhythm Interactions

Your body is constantly processing rhythm interactions. Learning to read these signals helps you understand what's happening.

What Positive Interaction Feels Like

When rhythms align and support each other, ease and flow emerge. Decisions come without forcing. Ideas arise without effort. Like swimming with the current instead of against it.

Time feels right. Not checking the clock constantly. Hours pass without notice or minutes don't drag.

Bodies soften. Shoulders drop, breathing deepens, faces relax. Watch a group when rhythms align—everyone simultaneously softens.

Natural creativity blooms. Solutions emerge without brainstorming. Innovation happens without forced "ideation."

Sustainable energy flows. Not the forced high of caffeine or deadline panic, but sustainable vitality.

I watched a book club accidentally find perfect rhythm alignment—monthly gathering after solo reading, during natural energy rise, at autumn's beginning. The discussion went three hours past normal. Nobody noticed. Ideas built on ideas. Everyone left energized rather than drained.

What Negative Interaction Feels Like

When rhythms conflict, everything takes effort. Opening your laptop feels like lifting weights. Starting the meeting requires tremendous will.

Time distorts. Minutes feel like hours. You check time constantly. Or hours vanish but nothing happened.

Bodies contract. Tension everywhere—jaw, shoulders, stomach. Headaches appear. People unconsciously lean away from each other.

Creativity blocks. No flow, no emergence, no natural solutions. Every idea feels forced or flat.

Energy depletes. Every minute drains reserves. You leave more exhausted than you arrived.

The neighborhood association scheduled meetings Sunday evenings—dispersal time plus falling energy plus dissolving weekend. Attendance dropped from forty to twelve. Those who came looked miserable.

They moved to Tuesday evenings—workweek gathering time, energy still present, creating energy. Attendance recovered immediately.

Diagnostic Questions

When exhausted, ask yourself these primary diagnostics. What movement does my body want right now? What movement is this group demanding? Where specifically is the mismatch?

For scale identification, consider whether this is an hourly conflict (right now needs versus demands), daily conflict (today's rhythm versus requirements), or weekly conflict (this week's pattern versus obligations).

For conflict mapping, determine if this is within one group or across groups, same timescale or different timescales.

Practical Prioritization

When multiple rhythms conflict, prioritize strategically.

1. Fix BREATH First

You can't do anything if you can't breathe. A group stuck in chronic gathering has no space to address other rhythms.

The Williams family discovered this—overscheduled (TIDE), exhausted (PULSE), and never apart (BREATH). They focused solely on creating dispersal time first. From that breathing space, they could address other patterns.

2. Address PULSE Second

Need sustainable energy to work on anything else. Can't solve completion issues when stuck in chronic rising.

3. Tackle TIDE Third

Creation and dissolution require both breathing room and sustainable energy. Most complex rhythm to shift because it involves grieving (dissolution) and risk (creation).

Leverage Point Analysis

Alternative approach—find the one shift that creates cascade effects.

Marcus discovered his commute was the leverage point. Ninety minutes each way on the highway meant forced immobility (couldn't disperse), podcast intensity (couldn't let energy fall), and transition inability (couldn't dissolve work before home). Switching to train let him walk, choose rest, and create transition ritual. That single shift cascaded through everything.

Integration Practice

The three movements aren't separate. They're one complex rhythm expressing itself in three ways. Your body demonstrates this with every breath—inhale gathers air while energy rises and creates oxygen exchange; exhale disperses air as energy falls and dissolves carbon dioxide.

This week, practice recognizing interactions.

Step 1: Choose one exhausting moment. Not general exhaustion but specific time—like Thursday evenings or Sunday mornings.

Step 2: Map the conflicts. What does your body want? What do groups demand? Which movements conflict?

Step 3: Name without solving. Just observe for one week. Say aloud, "This is rhythm conflict."

Step 4: Notice experiments. What happens when timing accidentally shifts? When someone's absent? Watch for natural experiments life provides.

Remember—you're not trying to eliminate all conflicts. You're learning to recognize them. Sometimes you'll choose group rhythm over personal rhythm—that's conscious choice, not unconscious violation.

Close your eyes for ten seconds. Feel your breath naturally rising and falling. Feel your heartbeat's rhythm. Now open your eyes and feel the room's rhythm. Feel the building's rhythm. Notice where they align. Notice where they conflict. That noticing—that's where everything begins.

Now that you recognize how rhythms interact and conflict, you need practices to unstick them. Simple experiments that create space for rhythm to return.

PART III: RELEASE

New Rhythm, New Life

R ecognition becomes restoration. Understanding shifts to practice.

You've gathered the evidence—exhaustion in your shoulders, spaces that suffocate or breathe, patterns repeating everywhere. You've paused to understand how groups naturally move. Now comes release—letting go of what doesn't work and allowing natural rhythm to return.

Chapter 6: Simple practices for unsticking patterns. Five-minute experiments that create cascading change.

Chapter 7: Real groups finding their rhythm—families, friendships, communities from across Upstate New York.

Chapter 8: Not everyone has equal access to rhythm restoration. Power determines who sets rhythms and who must follow them.

The epilogue returns to you with new recognition. You can't unsee these patterns now.

That's where everything begins—recognizing what prevents natural rhythm from returning.

Six

Recognizing What's Stuck

T he moment you name a stuck pattern, something shifts.
    Not because naming is magical. Because recognition stops the fight. Your body can finally stop trying to tell you something's wrong—you've heard it.

Watching groups transform through simple recognition, I've learned this—you don't need to fix the rhythm. You need to recognize what's stuck. The rhythm wants to flow. It just needs you to stop preventing what's already trying to happen.

Recognition Is Often Enough

A healthcare team: twelve nurses, three years of mounting tension, everyone exhausted. Administration had tried everything—team building, communication workshops, schedule changes. Nothing helped.

After watching for three days, I said during their afternoon huddle, "You're stuck in chronic gathering. You never actually disperse."

Silence.

Then one nurse said, "Oh my god. We're never alone. Even on break, we're in the same break room. Even off shift, we're in the group text. We're always together."

Within minutes—without any instruction from me—they started planning. Separate break spaces. Scheduled solo documentation time. A group text that could be muted without guilt.

I didn't tell them what to do. I just named what their bodies already knew. Recognition created space for rhythm to return.

Three months later, the team that almost disbanded from tension had become one of the hospital's strongest units. Not from team building. From recognizing they needed to breathe.

This isn't unique to workplaces. The Rodriguez family had been suffocating in forced togetherness for years—every meal together, every errand together, no one ever alone. During a particularly tense dinner, their teenage son said, "We never breathe. We're always breathing each other's air."

That single observation changed everything. Without any formal intervention, family members started taking walks alone. Mom began grocery shopping solo. Dad found reasons to work in the garage. The suffocation lifted not through planned practices but through recognition alone. The pattern, once named, began to shift.

Micro-Practices by Movement

Based on patterns I've observed across hundreds of groups, here are practices that create space for rhythm to return. Each takes less than five minutes. Your body will know which ones to try.

For BREATH (Gathering-Dispersing) Stuck

If You Can't Disperse (Chronic Gathering)

The Five-Minute Solo (Universal)

During any gathering—family dinner, friend meetup, team meeting—one person simply stands up and says, "I need five minutes," then walks outside. No explanation. No activity. Just five minutes alone.

The Nakamura family tried this. First time, everyone panicked. "Are you okay?" By week two, others started taking their five minutes. By month two, the family that had been suffocating in forced togetherness could actually enjoy being together.

Twenty minutes would be better. But five minutes of actual dispersing can shift an entire group's rhythm.

The No-Show Option (Friends/Community)

Your group that meets every week? Institute a no-show option. Once a month, anyone can skip without explanation. No guilt. No follow-up texts. Just absence accepted.

When the hiking group tried this, they thought everyone would abuse it. Instead, people used it rarely but crucially—when their bodies truly needed dispersing. The group stabilized instead of hemorrhaging members.

Protected Deep Work (Workplace)

Two days per week, no meetings before noon. No Slack. No "quick syncs." Real dispersing into individual work. Not remote work where you're still gathered digitally—actual solo time.

The design firm resisted this. "Collaboration is our culture!" But when they tried it, creativity increased. People brought better ideas to afternoon gatherings because they'd had morning dispersion.

If You Can't Gather (Chronic Dispersing)

Conscious Arrival (Universal)

Before anything else—phones away, agenda paused—acknowledge each person's presence. Three seconds of genuine recognition per person. Eye contact, verbal greeting, whatever fits your culture.

A remote team that met quarterly was going through motions without ever arriving. Three seconds of genuine acknowledgment per person changed everything. Scattered became coherent.

Device-Free Hour (Friends/Community)

One hour of any gathering, all devices go in a box. Not silent. Not face down. Actually away.

A book club had been meeting for two years but never really connecting. One device-free meeting changed their entire dynamic. "We finally met each other," one member said.

Meeting-Free Mornings (Workplace)

Nothing scheduled before noon on specific days. Not even "optional" gatherings. Protected time for deep work that naturally creates hunger for afternoon gathering.

Teams that protect mornings report afternoon meetings become more productive. People choose to gather because they've had time apart. Most workplaces make this impossible—calendar systems automatically fill empty time, "collaboration" metrics punish absence, being unavailable reads as not being a "team player."

For PULSE (Rising-Falling) Stuck

If You Can't Fall (Chronic Rising)

Empty Saturdays (Universal)

Nothing scheduled. No activities. No errands that could wait. Just empty time.

The Kumar family documented this. Week one was chaos—kids didn't know what to do. Week four, creativity emerged. Week eight, the anxious family found their ground.

Fallow Months (Community/Volunteer)

Pick two months a year—August and December work well—when your organization does nothing. No campaigns. No meetings. Optional participation only.

The environmental group thought this would kill momentum. Instead, their most innovative campaign emerged the January after their first fallow December. Rest enabled creation that constant action couldn't.

Valley Weeks (Workplace)

After every major project completion, declare a valley week. Only maintenance tasks. No new initiatives. No strategy. Just gentle work—documentation, organization, cleaning up.

The tech company discovered teams that took valley weeks produced better work in subsequent peaks.

If You Can't Rise (Chronic Falling)

One Good Thing (Universal)

Begin every gathering naming something that didn't break. Not forced positivity. Just recognition that something works. "The coffee is warm." "We all showed up."

A medical team in chronic depression started this. Tiny acknowledgments. Week three, genuine energy began returning.

Two-Minute Music (Friends/Community)

Two minutes of music that moves. Not background—foreground. Everyone stops and listens or moves.

The nonprofit in permanent low energy tried this. By week three, people were arriving early to hear what song would play. Energy that had been flat for two years began to pulse.

Stand and Deliver (Workplace)

Important announcements delivered standing. Meetings start with everyone standing for first five minutes. Physical rising enables energetic rising.

The office where everyone was emotionally flat instituted standing check-ins. The physical elevation helped energy rise. Bodies taught what minds couldn't force.

For TIDE (Creating-Dissolving) Stuck

If You Can't Dissolve (Chronic Creating)

Gratitude Release (Universal)

Choose one thing everyone secretly dreads—a tradition, a meeting format, a group text. Gather specifically to thank it and release it. "We release this with gratitude for what it gave us."

The O'Brien family released mandatory Sunday dinners that had become forced performances. Spontaneous Sunday gatherings sometimes replaced them. The voluntary had vitality the mandatory lacked.

Completion Ceremonies (Community/Volunteer)

Monthly, any program ready to end can request a completion ceremony. Not failure—completion. Share what was attempted, celebrate what was achieved, formally dissolve with gratitude.

The temple had forty-three programs, most zombies. Monthly completion ceremonies let twenty-eight programs die with dignity in one year. New programs emerged organically in the space created.

Sunset Protocols (Workplace)

Every project, committee, and initiative gets an expiration date. Three months, six months, one year—whatever makes sense. To continue requires active renewal, not passive continuation.

The nonprofit went from sixty-seven initiatives to twelve using sunset protocols. Conscious completion creates focus.

If You Can't Create (Chronic Dissolving)

Protect One Thing (Universal)

Choose one pattern that won't change. One meeting time. One tradition. One process. Mark it explicitly as protected.

The startup in constant pivot protected Friday afternoon show-and-tell. No matter what else changed, that remained. It became the heartbeat around which other patterns could evolve.

Name What Works (Friends/Community)

Before changing anything, name three things actually working. Write them down. Post them visibly.

The school district in constant reform started requiring this. Before any new initiative, name three things working in current system. It slowed the chronic dissolution.

Anchor Meetings (Workplace)

One meeting that never moves, never changes format, never gets "optimized." The structural stability allows everything else to evolve.

The agency in constant restructure protected their Monday morning creative review. Same time, same format, for five years. That one anchor allowed radical experimentation elsewhere.

When Multiple Movements Stuck

Most exhaustion isn't from single rhythm violation—it's from multiple movements stuck simultaneously.

Jason the parent from Chapter 3 was experiencing chronic gathering (always visible) plus forced rising (performing energy) plus nothing completes (endless tasks). Total system breakdown pending.

The design firm before transformation had chronic gathering (open office) plus chronic rising (sprint culture) plus chronic creating (zombie projects). Burnout factory exporting exhaustion home.

Marcus the volunteer faced chronic rising (permanent emergency) plus no completion (campaigns never end) plus forced gathering (crisis meetings). The result was dissociation.

Your body experiences these as compound violations. That's why single solutions fail—"self-care" can't fix chronic gathering while forced rising continues. "Boundaries" can't address accumulation while dissolution is prevented. You're trying to bail water while multiple leaks continue.

The Universal Practice

Whatever pattern you've recognized, the practice is the same.

Notice where something feels stuck. Feel it in your body. Where does the stuckness live?

Name it out loud to someone. "We're stuck in chronic gathering." "Our energy never falls." "Nothing ever completes here."

Try one micro-practice. Five minutes maximum. Don't announce it as an experiment. Just do it.

Watch what shifts. Sometimes it's immediate—the room feels different. Sometimes gradual—three weeks later, someone says, "Something's different."

You're not forcing change. You're removing obstacles to rhythm that wants to return.

When Rhythm Can't Be Restored

Sometimes recognition reveals that rhythm can't be restored because the group shouldn't exist—or because you lack power to change it.

Recognizing Wrong Fit

Some groups aren't meant to sync. Your body knows the difference between difficult and wrong.

Difficult feels like growth—challenging but possible. Wrong feels like violence—forcing something that resists at cellular level.

The food co-op tried every practice I've mentioned. Nothing helped. Finally someone said, "What if we're not supposed to be a group?"

They disbanded. Within six months, everyone had found groups that actually fit. The co-op had been a gathering point, not a destination.

Leaving With Dignity

When rhythm can't be restored, leaving becomes necessary.

First comes internal release. Stop forcing yourself to match the wrong rhythm. Let your energy withdraw naturally.

Second, clean communication. "This isn't working for me" is complete. You don't need elaborate justification.

Third, actual leaving. Not half-leaving where you stay physically but check out emotionally. Complete departure creates space for what fits.

My second soccer team taught me this. We weren't meant to breathe together. The exhaustion wasn't from soccer—it was from forcing connection that didn't exist. Some groups are mismatches. Leaving is data, not failure.

Power and Practice

Sometimes rhythm can't be restored because you lack power to change it.

Who can't do these practices?

The single parent working three jobs can't create "empty Saturdays"—every minute is survival. The low-wage worker can't refuse the meeting schedule—attendance is monitored, absence is punished. The person in an abusive relationship can't announce "I need five minutes alone"—dispersing might trigger violence. The hourly worker can't push back on impossible demands—survival depends on keeping the job.

What makes practices inaccessible?

Economic constraint means you can't afford to work less, can't risk job loss, need multiple incomes to survive.

Safety issues mean dispersing isn't safe, naming problems risks retaliation, trying changes could escalate danger.

Structural power means you're not the one who sets meeting times, determines workload, controls schedules. Others decide your rhythm, you must comply.

What's the alternative when you lack power?

Recognition itself becomes the practice. Naming to yourself, "This exhaustion isn't my failure, it's structural violence." Finding micro-moments where you can—breathing in the bathroom, thirty seconds of stillness, the walk from parking lot. Connecting with others experiencing same violations—shared recognition reduces isolation. Sometimes organizing collectively for change. Sometimes just surviving until conditions shift.

Validation matters when change isn't possible. Your exhaustion is accurate data about imposed rhythm violations, not personal weakness. Your body is keeping score of structural impossibility, not individual failure.

Chapter 8 addresses this directly—who gets to set rhythm, who must follow it, and what changes when you lack power. Not everyone has equal access to rhythm restoration. Recognizing this isn't giving up—it's being honest about what individual practices can and can't address.

The Body's Wisdom

After years observing stuck patterns and rhythm restoration, here's what I know—your body is wiser than any framework.

That tight chest knows you're stuck in chronic gathering before your mind admits it. That flat feeling knows energy needs to fall before you give permission. That overwhelm knows things need to complete before you can name what.

The micro-practices aren't solutions. They're experiments. Your body will tell you which ones to try, how long to sustain them, when to stop.

Some groups will transform through recognition alone. Some will need sustained practice. Some will reveal themselves as mismatches. Some will show you that power, not practice, is what needs to change. Your body knows the difference.

This Week's Experiment

Pick one group you're part of. Just one.

Spend three days noticing where rhythm feels stuck. Don't judge or fix. Just notice.

Day four, name it to someone. "I think we're stuck in chronic gathering."

Day five, try one micro-practice. Five minutes or less. See what's possible.

Day six and seven, watch. What's different? What does your body tell you?

If nothing shifts, that's data too. Maybe this group can't change. Maybe you lack power to change it. Maybe it's the wrong group entirely. All of this is valuable information.

That's all. One week. One group. One small experiment.

Sometimes that's where everything begins.

Stand up right now. Shake your whole body for ten seconds. Hard. Let everything move. Now stop. Feel the stillness that follows. That shift from movement to stillness—that's rhythm returning. Your body just did in ten seconds what your groups need to remember.

Tomorrow you'll see stuck patterns everywhere. Don't try to fix them all. Just pick one. The smallest shift in rhythm can transform an entire group. But it starts with recognition. Name what's stuck. The rhythm already knows how to flow.

Seven

When Groups Remember

I t doesn't happen all at once. Groups don't suddenly remember they're human. The shift is gradual, sometimes barely visible, until one day everyone realizes—we can breathe again.

Transformation follows consistent patterns. Not through dramatic interventions or organizational overhauls. But through small recognitions that accumulate into fundamental shift, like snow gathering grain by grain until the landscape transforms.

This chapter shares stories of groups that remembered. Not perfect groups—there are none. But groups that recognized their stuck patterns and created space for rhythm to return. Important to note—these groups had certain advantages. Leadership with authority to make changes, economic stability to experiment, psychological safety to name problems. Not every group has these conditions. The transformations that follow aren't blueprints for everyone—they're examples of what becomes possible when power and recognition align.

The Family That Found Its Breath

Remember the Okonkwo-Johnsons from Chapter 4? The family that did everything together—every errand, every meal, every evening. They thought togetherness meant love. Their bodies knew it meant suffocation.

Ade's shoulders stayed raised, braced against invasion that never stopped. David sat in his car ten minutes before entering the house, stealing moments of solitude in the driveway. Teenage Kimi lingered in the library after school, breathing air that belonged to no one else. Eight-year-old Kai had daily meltdowns that therapists wanted to medicate.

The change began with Ade's twenty-minute experiment. Every evening after dinner, each family member would disperse for twenty minutes. No explanation, no activities, just twenty minutes alone.

Week one was chaos. "Where are you going?" "What's wrong?" "Are we falling apart?" Kai cried the first night David walked outside. The forced togetherness had become so normal that separation felt like abandonment.

But Ade held firm. Twenty minutes. Every evening. Non-negotiable.

Week two, something shifted. Kai stopped panicking when adults left the room. Started using the twenty minutes to build elaborate Lego creations—alone, in focused silence. Kimi put down the phone and started sketching—real art, not social media scrolling.

By month two, the twenty minutes had evolved organically. Sometimes it was fifteen minutes, sometimes thirty. Sometimes Kai and David dispersed together to the backyard but did separate activities—parallel solitude. The dispersing had become natural, not forced.

But here's what really changed—the quality of their gathering transformed. When you can disperse, gathering becomes voluntary. When gathering is voluntary, it becomes vital.

They'd come back together for evening activities differently. Hungrier for each other's presence. Stories bubbled up that hadn't been shared in months. David laughed—actually laughed—instead of performing enjoyment. Kimi started sharing their art. Kai's meltdowns stopped completely.

Six months later, when I visited them again, the transformation was subtle but profound.

"We still do most things together," Ade explained. "But now it's chosen, not chronic. We gather because we want to, not because we're afraid of what separation means."

The family had developed natural breathing patterns. Morning gathering at breakfast felt energized because everyone had slept in their own rhythm. After-school dispersing happened automatically—everyone finding their corner before reconvening for dinner. Evening dispersing had become sacred time, protected without discussion.

They'd also discovered something crucial—different family members needed different amounts of dispersing. Kimi, the introvert, needed an hour daily. Kai needed just twenty minutes but needed it absolutely. David needed his morning solitude. Ade needed her evening walk around the neighborhood. They stopped trying to synchronize everyone's rhythm and started honoring individual needs within family structure.

"We thought constant togetherness proved we were a good family," David reflected. "Now we know that letting each other breathe is what makes us a good family."

This transformation was possible because the Okonkwo-Johnsons had economic stability to be home evenings, a safe neighborhood for walks, and family cohesion strong enough to experiment. Not every family has these conditions.

The Friend Group Revival

The Wednesday Walking Group had been withering for two years. What started as Juliet's lifeline during divorce had become everyone's burden. Eight years of weekly walks at the park, same six women, same trail, same time. The consistency that once saved Juliet now imprisoned everyone.

The group text grew tense. "Can't make it" triggered guilt spirals. "See you Wednesday!" felt like threats. Rachel got tension headaches Tuesday nights. Lisa double-booked "accidentally." Maria claimed injuries to sit on benches.

Juliet finally said what everyone felt during a particularly cold March walk. "I love you all, but I'm drowning in obligation."

The silence wasn't shock. It was relief, visible in the vapor of their breath.

But relief quickly turned to conflict. Eight years of forced gathering had created resentments nobody knew they carried. "If it's such a burden—" "Why didn't you say something earlier—" "I thought this meant something to you—"

The hurt was real. These women had walked through divorce, cancer, job loss, teenage crises together. How could something so meaningful have become so exhausting?

Maria broke the tension. "We confused consistency with connection. We turned friendship into forced labor."

The solution emerged slowly, like spring arriving. Monthly meetings instead of weekly. With a crucial addition—the no-show option. Once a month, anyone could skip without explanation. No guilt. No follow-up texts. Just absence accepted.

The resistance was fierce. "Monthly? We'll drift apart." "No-show means nobody will come." "This is how friendships die."

But they were desperate enough to try. The friendship was dying anyway from chronic obligation.

First monthly meeting in April—four of six showed up. The two who didn't sent simple heart emojis—no explanations, no apologies. The four who gathered? They walked for two hours instead of one, stopping at the lake, sitting on rocks, actually talking instead of just covering miles. Real stories emerged. Deep laughter returned. They remembered why they'd chosen each other.

"I hadn't realized how much I'd been editing myself," Lisa admitted. "Performing happiness when I was exhausted. Showing up when I needed to be alone."

Second month—all six came. The month apart had created genuine desire to gather. They had things to share, stories that had ripened in solitude.

By month six, something unexpected had evolved. They still met monthly as a full group. But smaller configurations gathered spontaneously—two for coffee, three for a movie, four for hiking. The forced structure had dissolved into natural affinity.

The group text transformed too. Instead of logistics and guilt, it became a space for spontaneous sharing—photos from solo walks, quotes that resonated, moments of beauty. Connection without chronic gathering.

Two years later, the Wednesday Walking Group is stronger than ever. They walk monthly, sometimes more, sometimes less. The no-show option gets used rarely but crucially—when someone's body truly needs solitude, they take it without explanation.

"We thought friendship meant never letting go," Juliet told me. "We were holding on so tight we were crushing each other. Turns out friendship means knowing when to hold tight and when to release."

These friends had the social capital to renegotiate relationship norms and enough security in the friendship to risk change. Not all friendships have that foundation.

The Community Awakening

The Riverside Neighborhood Association had burned through seven presidents in five years. Same pattern every time—initial enthusiasm, gradual overwhelm, complete burnout, resignation.

When Mx. Jamie Chen took over, they were the eighth attempt. But Jamie recognized something others hadn't—the neighborhood was stuck in chronic gathering.

Monthly meetings had become weekly. Committees had spawned subcommittees. The WhatsApp group required daily engagement. Every broken streetlight triggered three meetings. Every community issue demanded immediate gathering.

"I felt like I was breathing for the entire neighborhood," Jamie told me. "Six families doing all the work while three hundred watched and occasionally criticized."

The breaking point came during that Tuesday night "emergency meeting" about holiday decorations in November. Three people showed up to the community center. Jamie looked at the empty chairs and started crying. Not dramatic sobs—just quiet tears of recognition.

"We're killing this community with togetherness," Jamie said to the empty room.

The two other attendees—Tom, who ran the safety committee, and Maria, who managed social events—sat in silence. Then Tom said, "I haven't enjoyed a neighborhood event in two years. I just feel obligated to organize them."

That honest moment changed everything.

Jamie made a radical decision—dissolve everything except quarterly meetings. No committees. No WhatsApp group. No group chat. No subcommittees. No working groups. Just four gatherings a year, optional attendance.

The resistance was immediate and vicious. "You're destroying everything we've built!" "The neighborhood will fall apart!" "This is abandonment of leadership!"

But Jamie had positional authority and used it. "We're not destroying anything. We're letting it breathe."

First quarterly meeting after the dissolution? Twelve families came—double the recent average for weekly meetings. Without the burden of constant engagement, people were curious again. Without forced connection, genuine interest emerged.

But here's what nobody expected—the neighborhood became more connected, not less.

Without formal committees, organic connections emerged. Parents with young children found each other at the playground and organized playdates—no committee needed. Gardeners started sharing tools over fences—no structure required. Elderly residents began morning walks together—no one managing them.

"We'd been trying to manufacture community through meetings," reflected Tom. "But community was already there. We were just suffocating it with structure."

Six months later, thirty families attended the spring gathering. Not from obligation but from genuine desire—three months of dispersing had made them hungry for their neighbors.

The quarterly meetings had energy that weekly meetings never achieved. People came with stories to share, connections to celebrate, natural enthusiasm instead of forced participation. Issues that actually needed community input got addressed. Everything else sorted itself organically.

A year later, Riverside is one of the most connected neighborhoods in the city. Not through programs or committees, but through natural rhythm. Neighbors help each other because they want to, not because they're assigned to a committee. Events happen spontaneously—someone starts a barbecue, others join if they feel like it.

"We thought community meant constant gathering," Jamie reflected. "But constant gathering was killing community. We had to let it disperse to let it live."

Jamie had the positional authority to dissolve committees and the social capital to weather criticism.

Not everyone in the neighborhood could have made these changes.

You might notice these stories aren't from workplaces. That's intentional. Families, friendships, and communities are where most readers have direct agency to experiment. Workplace transformation often requires positional authority most readers don't have—which Chapter 8 addresses directly.

What Actually Changes

When groups remember they're human, the changes are subtle but profound.

Meeting quality transforms. When gathering is chosen, not chronic, people arrive present. Energy flows naturally rather than being forced. Real connection replaces performed proximity.

Exhaustion shifts to vitality. Not perfect energy—human energy. Sometimes high, sometimes low. But flowing rather than forced. Bodies stop rebelling because they're no longer being violated.

Conflict changes character. Groups still disagree, but not from rhythm violation. When everyone can breathe, petty tensions dissolve. Real differences can be addressed without the static of exhaustion.

Natural leaders emerge. Not through exhaustion-based default—whoever can sustain chronic violation longest—but through genuine capacity matching actual need. Leadership becomes expression of rhythm, not evidence of endurance.

Innovation returns. Creativity requires rhythm—gathering inspiration, dispersing to process, rising to create, falling to integrate. Groups that remember their rhythm remember how to innovate.

The Bridge to Power

These transformations happened because people had certain conditions—economic stability, social capital, positional authority. The Okonkwo-Johnsons could experiment with evening rhythm because they had stable schedules. The Walking Group could renegotiate because they had friendship security. Jamie could dissolve committees because they had presidential authority.

Not everyone has these conditions. The practices work when you have agency to implement them. When you don't, the work becomes different. That's what we need to address now—who gets to set rhythm, who must follow it, and what changes when you lack power. Because here's what these three stories don't show—what happens when you're the hourly worker, not the family head? When you're the newest member, not the group founder? When you're the one without authority, safety, or choice? Recognition matters there too—but it works differently.

These groups weren't special. They just recognized what was stuck and created space for rhythm to return. Your group might be one recognition away from remembering it's human. But that recognition requires conditions—safety, agency, power—that aren't equally distributed. The next chapter addresses what happens when those conditions don't exist.

Eight

Who Gets to Set the Rhythm

Reading about the Okonkwo-Johnsons instituting twenty-minute dispersals, you might have thought: "That's great—but what if one parent works three jobs and is never home? What if there's an abusive partner who won't allow anyone to leave? What if dispersing isn't safe?"

Reading about the neighborhood association reducing to quarterly meetings, you might have wondered: "What if you're not the president? What if speaking up about rhythm violations risks your safety in your community? What if you don't have the social capital to suggest radical change?"

Reading about the design firm protecting solo work time, you might have asked: "What if you're hourly and can't afford to work fewer days? What if you're the only woman and already fighting for credibility? What if your manager demands constant availability and you can't risk your job?"

These questions have probably been rising throughout this book. It's time to address them directly.

This chapter addresses directly what earlier chapters acknowledged—rhythm isn't equally accessible to everyone. Power determines who can set the rhythm, who must follow it, and who has no choice at all.

I see patterns. But my position—white, male, educated, economically stable—affects what I can see and what remains invisible. This book emerges from and primarily speaks to those with enough stability to worry about "rhythm" rather than survival. That's both its limitation and its specific usefulness. This chapter names some of what I've missed or understated.

Notice what happened in your body when you read those opening questions. Did you feel relief that someone finally named the limitations? Tension that I took so long to address them? Both? That reaction is data about your relationship to power and rhythm.

Who Gets to Disperse

When I suggest families need dispersing time, I'm assuming a safe home to disperse to. Agency to be alone without consequence. Economic stability that allows unplugged time. Physical safety during solitude. Social permission to prioritize self.

Many people don't have these.

The Gig Worker

James drives for three different apps—rideshare, delivery, whatever pays. His phone controls his rhythm entirely. When I talk about "groups needing to breathe," he pulls up his apps. "See these acceptance rates? Drop below 80% and the algorithm punishes you. I can't disperse. I can't let my energy fall. The app decides when I work, and if I don't accept immediately, I lose income."

His exhaustion isn't fixable through micro-practices. It's built into platform capitalism that extracts maximum labor while providing minimum security. What James needs isn't rhythm recognition—it's worker protections and algorithmic accountability.J

A Person in an Abusive Relationship

When I suggest "five minutes alone outside," I'm assuming that's safe. For someone in an abusive relationship, announcing "I need five minutes" might trigger violence. Dispersing isn't rest—it's risk.

The rhythm violation isn't that the family can't disperse. It's that one person uses power to control others' movement. No amount of micro-practices fixes this. What's needed is safety, resources to leave, and systems that protect survivors.

The Low-Wage Worker

"Protected solo time" assumes you can refuse work demands without losing your job. "Meeting-free mornings" assumes you have leverage. "No-show options" assume absence is permitted.

For people earning low wages in retail, food service, caregiving, or warehouse work—whose survival depends on perfect attendance, accepting every shift, never saying no—rhythm work isn't just unavailable, suggesting it is cruel. Their bodies know they're stuck. They don't need recognition. They need living wages, predictable schedules, and labor protections.

If you saw yourself in these examples, the practices in Chapter 6 assume choices you don't have.

What I can offer is validation that your exhaustion is accurate information about structural violence. Language for what's being done to you (forced rhythm violations). Recognition that your body's rebellion isn't weakness—it's wisdom refusing to adapt to the intolerable.

Sometimes rhythm work isn't about finding your group's natural flow. It's about identifying which rhythms are being forced on you by power, naming that clearly, and connecting with others experiencing similar violations.

Power operates everywhere. The child who can't escape their overscheduled life. The community member whose voice doesn't carry weight. The friend who can't reshape group norms without social capital.

But nowhere is power more visible, more systematic, more structurally embedded than in workplaces—particularly corporations and large institutions. This isn't about individual leaders being cruel. It's about how extractive systems create conditions where rhythm violations become organizational features. Quarterly earnings demand constant rising. Competitive pressure prevents completion. Efficiency metrics eliminate dispersing. Human exhaustion becomes an externalized cost.

Understanding how these structural dynamics operate in workplaces illuminates how power shapes rhythm everywhere else. Not because work matters more than family or community, but because workplace structures make the mechanisms undeniable.

Who Gets to Set Organizational Rhythm

The workplace transformations in Chapter 7—valley weeks, protected dispersing, completion ceremonies—required something I didn't name: power. Usually held by people with formal authority, social capital, or organizational influence.

The creative director who protected Friday descent time? She had budget authority and team leadership. The nursing unit that took real breaks? The unit director championed it. The design firm that went to two-day solo weeks? The founders decided.

The CEO who reads about 'valley weeks' in this book can institute them tomorrow. The contract cleaner in the same building, experiencing identical chronic rising, has zero power to create valleys. Both feel the exhaustion in their bodies. Only one can change the schedule. This difference—between those who set rhythms and those who must endure them—is what this chapter addresses.

What about the administrative assistant who knows the meeting schedule is suffocating but can't change it? The junior developer who sees the chronic urgency but fears speaking up? The cleaning staff who experience the building's held breath but aren't in decision-making spaces? The contract worker who's not included in "rhythm restoration" conversations?

Power doesn't just determine who can change rhythm. Power operates through rhythm control.

Digital platforms force chronic gathering. You're never allowed to disperse because attention extraction requires constant connection. "Always on" isn't accident—it's the business model.

Precarious employment forces chronic rising. Can't show weakness, can't rest, can't acknowledge natural descent. The gig economy monetizes the elimination of valleys.

Extractive organizations prevent completion. Projects that never end, initiatives that accumulate endlessly. Completion would reveal how little gets genuinely finished. Chronic creation hides low actual impact.

The modern workplace has become the site where rhythm violations concentrate most intensely, then spread to every other domain of life. The open office that eliminates privacy? Now your home is an open office through constant digital connection. The sprint culture that denies valleys? Now your family runs in sprint mode—every child activity optimized, every weekend productive. The project management that prevents completion? Now your friendships have KPIs and your volunteer work has metrics.

Extractive systems didn't just allow rhythm violations—they created structural incentives for their elimination. Quarterly earnings demand constant rising. Competitive pressure prevents completion. Efficiency metrics eliminate dispersing. And those structural patterns now shape how we organize families, friendships, communities. The exhausted parent managing their home like a startup? They learned that logic at work. The friend group with mandatory weekly meetings? They're reproducing office culture. The community organization in permanent crisis mode? They've internalized corporate urgency.

These aren't rhythm violations to fix through micro-practices. They're features of systems structured to extract maximum value while distributing minimum power.

Why do workplaces violate rhythm so systematically? Because rhythmic humans are less extractable. Bodies that need rest can't work 80 hours. Groups that complete projects don't generate endless billable hours. People who disperse can't be surveilled constantly. Market dynamics reveal that eliminating human rhythm increases short-term extraction—even as it destroys long-term sustainability. The exhaustion isn't the goal, but it's the inevitable result of systems structured to maximize extraction regardless of cost to humans.

Seeing rhythm violations as power operations changes the work.

At the **individual level**, your exhaustion isn't personal failure or just rhythm mismatch. It might be accurate perception of exploitation. Trust that. Act accordingly (which might mean organizing, not optimizing).

At the **team level**, rhythm restoration might require confronting management, not just adjusting practices. "We need valley weeks" becomes a power negotiation, not just a wellness intervention.

At the **organizational level**, sustainable rhythm might require structural change—ownership models, decision-making power, resource distribution. Not just "culture change."

At the **systemic level**, some rhythm violations require policy—labor law, worker protection, economic redistribution. Individual and group-level work isn't enough.

This doesn't invalidate the practices in Chapter 6, but it contextualizes them—these work when you have power to implement them. When you don't, different work is needed.

Cultural Context and Different Exhaustions

When I "discovered" that groups need to breathe, I was recognizing something my own culture had forgotten. I come from traditions that chose extraction over rhythm—systems that traded human sustainability for the machinery of profit.

Indigenous communities around the world—including the Haudenosaunee here in this region—have maintained teachings about natural cycles and community rhythms for millennia. What I call discovery, many cultures call remembering what was never lost. Communities who experienced slavery, colonization, and systematic oppression developed their own complex practices around time, gathering, and preservation. This book doesn't attempt to explain those knowledge systems, which exist far beyond the patterns I describe.

When I write about "groups forgetting they're human," I need to be specific: I'm witnessing what happens in cultures built on extractive practices. The exhaustion I'm mapping emerges from systems that systematically eliminate human rhythm in service of productivity.

But not all exhaustion comes from forgetting. Some comes from having natural rhythms disrupted by force—through displacement, through labor extraction, through cultural suppression. These are different exhaustions requiring different responses. What my culture forgot, others were prevented from practicing. What we eliminated for efficiency, others had stolen through violence.

The patterns in this book—BREATH, PULSE, TIDE—describe what I've observed in my context. They might resonate with your experience or they might not. Use what serves you. Trust what your body knows about your own exhaustion, your own rhythms, your own context.

Whether exhaustion comes from forgetting or from forced violation, it's real. It lives in bodies. And recognizing it as structural rather than personal is where transformation begins.

When Rhythm Work Serves Power

There's a shadow to everything I've written—this book could become another tool for avoiding what actually needs to change.

I've watched it happen. Organizations discover "rhythm restoration" and use it to extract more labor, not less. They offer meditation apps instead of living wages. Breathing exercises instead of breathing room. Valley hours instead of structural transformation.

Corporate "wellness" programs teach breathing techniques while maintaining extractive practices. "Do some yoga so you can work 80 hours!" The rhythm violation isn't addressed—just the symptoms.

"Self-care" industries sell rhythm restoration as individual responsibility. "You're exhausted because you don't have good boundaries!" No—maybe you're exhausted because you're working three jobs.

Organizational "culture initiatives" rename control as rhythm. "We're implementing mandatory fun!" or "Everyone must attend team-building!" Forced rhythm isn't natural rhythm.

Or the manager who reads this book, recognizes their team is stuck in chronic rising, but responds by giving everyone stress balls and meditation apps rather than addressing the impossible deadlines they're imposing.

I don't want this book used that way. But I can't control how it's used.

So I'll be explicit—if someone with power over you recommends this book as solution to exhaustion they're causing through extractive practices, that's co-optation. Trust your body. The solution might not be finding rhythm within exploitation—it might be refusing exploitation.

How to tell if rhythm work serves power versus challenges it?

Serves power when it puts responsibility on individuals to adapt, doesn't address resource distribution, maintains existing power structures, treats exhaustion as personal problem, positions rhythm as wellness benefit, doesn't name who controls the rhythm.

Challenges power when it names structural causes of rhythm violations, addresses who decides and who must comply, creates space for collective organizing, treats exhaustion as political information, positions rhythm as human right, redistributes control over rhythms.

Where does this book sit? Honestly—somewhere in between.

It provides individual and small-group tools (can be co-opted). It validates embodied knowing and resistance (can challenge power). It names patterns without always naming who enforces them (this chapter tries to correct that).

Use it how it serves. If it helps you find breathing room—good. If it helps you recognize what needs organizing against—also good. If it gets used to avoid addressing extraction—resist that.

Take a moment to feel into your own position. Where do you have power to set rhythm? Where must you follow others' rhythms? Where have you no choice at all? Your body knows the difference between these positions. Trust what it tells you.

What Changes With This Recognition

For Readers With Significant Power

If you're the creative director, the department head, the founder, the community leader with social capital, recognizing power changes your rhythm work. You're not just "facilitating natural flow." You're using positional authority to redistribute rhythm control.

Questions to ask—who in my organization can't say no to chronic gathering? Whose exhaustion am I benefiting from? What rhythm violations am I enforcing through my position? How might "rhythm restoration" actually give others more power? What am I willing to give up to make natural rhythm accessible to more people?

The practices in Chapter 6 work differently when you have power to implement them broadly. You're not just helping your group breathe—you're potentially shifting who controls breathing.

For Readers With Moderate Power

If you're middle management, community organizer, department member with some voice, you have constraints above and some authority below.

Rhythm work for you might mean protecting your team from rhythm violations imposed from above. Naming pattern violations in spaces where you have voice. Building coalitions with others in similar positions. Practicing rhythm restoration where you can while organizing for broader change. Being honest about what you can and can't shift.

For Readers With Little Structural Power

If you're an hourly worker, marginalized in your organization, survival-dependent on compliance, this chapter hopefully validates that the practices in Chapter 6 might not be available to you. That's not your failure.

What might still serve is recognizing forced rhythm violations for what they are (structural violence, not your inadequacy). Finding whatever breathing room is possible without risk. Connecting with others experiencing similar violations (rhythm recognition as organizing tool). Trusting your body's rebellion as wisdom (it's not you—it's the system). Knowing your exhaustion is accurate information about what needs changing.

Power isn't binary (have it/don't have it). It's contextual. You might have power in one group, none in another.

Where you have power, use this book to redistribute rhythm control, not optimize your group's performance. Where you lack power, use this book to name what's being done to you, connect with others, and organize when possible.

The diagnostic tools in Chapter 6's "When Rhythm Can't Be Restored" section can help distinguish—is this rhythm I can address through practice, or structural violence requiring different work?

Either way, rhythm work happens within power structures. Naming that clearly changes the work from individual wellness to collective liberation.

The Rhythm We Might Share

Earlier, I suggested that recognition spreads—one person, one group at a time. That's true but incomplete.

What I should have also said is that some pattern spreads will be individual choices. Others will be collective organizing. Still others will require structural transformation.

The parent teaching their kid to disperse might create generational change.

The workers organizing for valley weeks might shift labor practices.

The community demanding affordable housing might make dispersal physically safe.

The movements redistributing wealth might make natural rhythm economically accessible.

The cultural projects decolonizing time might restore rhythms that were disrupted.

All of these are rhythm work. None are just individual practice.

After years observing how groups move, break, and sometimes heal, here's what I now understand—rhythm violations aren't equally distributed. Power determines who must violate their rhythm in service of others' comfort, profit, or control.

The exhausted single parent, the surveilled worker, the violence survivor, the low-wage laborer—their exhaustion isn't personal failure or even simple rhythm violation. It's the somatic cost of structural violence.

The executive who institutes valley weeks has different agency than the contract cleaner experiencing the same chronic rising. Both feel the exhaustion. Only one can change the schedule.

This doesn't invalidate the patterns I've observed. BREATH, PULSE, and TIDE still describe how human groups naturally move. But it contextualizes them—these rhythms flow freely only when power permits.

The workplace isn't just another context where rhythm violations occur. It's the engine driving rhythm violations everywhere else. When we normalize surveillance at work, we accept it at home. When we celebrate burnout professionally, we shame rest personally. When we prevent completion organizationally, we accumulate endlessly in every domain.

This is why organizational rhythm work matters beyond organizations. Transform workplace rhythms, and family rhythms might remember themselves. Challenge corporate chronic rising, and communities might rediscover valleys. The revolution might begin where the violations are most extreme—in the very organizations that perfected forgetting we're human.

Maybe the rhythm we share isn't just recognition spreading through exhausted bodies. Maybe it's also collective refusal, organized resistance, structural transformation, and reclamation of what was stolen.

This book has focused on the first. But it's incomplete without acknowledging the rest.

Put your hands over your heart. Feel it beating. That rhythm is yours—but only if you have safety, agency, and power to honor it. For many, the work isn't finding rhythm. It's fighting for the conditions that make rhythm possible. That fight—that's rhythm work too.

Epilogue

Now That You Know

Y ou can't unknow this.

Tomorrow, you'll walk into your kitchen and feel whether your family's morning rhythm flows or fights. You'll sit in a meeting and know immediately if the group is stuck in chronic gathering. You'll notice your friend group's exhaustion and recognize—maybe for the first time—that it's not personal failure but rhythm violation.

Your exhaustion is data. Your body sensing what your mind might deny—that the groups you're part of have forgotten they're human. Your body will keep teaching you, now that you know how to listen.

Put this book down. Stand up. Take the deepest breath you've taken today. Feel your lungs fill completely. Now exhale everything. Let your shoulders drop. Feel the space that opens when you release. That space—that's where new rhythm begins.

What Happens Tomorrow

Tomorrow, you might share one observation from this book. Not to teach, just to see if someone else recognizes it too.

At dinner, you might say, "I've been noticing we never really disperse. We're always together, even when we're apart."

At your book club, "What if we let this format die and see what wants to emerge?"

With an exhausted colleague at the office park, "What if the exhaustion isn't personal? What if it's the workplace rhythm that's broken?"

Watch their face change. Watch them exhale. Watch recognition dawn like morning light over water.

That's how it spreads—through bodies that recognize truth when they hear it. One conversation at a time. One group at a time. One small shift creating space for another.

Someone recognizes their team is stuck in chronic rising. They protect one valley hour. The shift is tiny but palpable. Team members carry something different home. A spouse notices, tries something similar. The pattern ripples in ways we can't track but can feel.

The Choice Ahead

For those with power to set rhythms—use this book to redistribute control, not optimize extraction. Create space for others to breathe.

For those without that power—use this book to name what's being done to you. Recognition itself is the beginning. Sometimes knowing why you're exhausted is the seed of transformation, even when immediate change isn't possible.

Some of you will go deeper. Especially those in workplaces—where rhythm violations are most systematic and most exportable—who want transformation tools beyond individual practice. Or those curious how consciousness itself organizes through groups. The exhaustion epidemic you now recognize might be information about larger cultural shifts.

But even if you do nothing except recognize—even if all you do is understand why you're tired—something has changed. You have language for what you've always felt. Permission to trust your body's knowing. Validation that the exhaustion is real, means something, and isn't your fault.

Close your eyes. Imagine one group you're part of finding its rhythm. Feel what would change. Hold that possibility. It lives in your body now.

Now We Begin

That first soccer team still teaches me—the one that breathed as one organism. They showed me rhythm can't be forced, only found.

The rhythm was always there—in bodies that breathe, in energy that cycles, in patterns that naturally compose and decompose.

You know this now. You can't unknow it.

And tomorrow—in some small way, in some small group—you might help rhythm return. One breath at a time. One recognition at a time. One group remembering it's human.

The revolution isn't coming. It's here—in every small group that finds its breath, every person who stops forcing machine rhythms onto human systems, every body that refuses what violates its nature. Especially in workplaces—those laboratories of rhythm violation—where transformation might begin. Because if we can remember we're human in the places that most systematically forgot—the organizations that engineered rhythm elimination—we might remember everywhere else too.

You're part of this now. Use it wisely. Share it gently. Let it work through you in whatever way feels right.

The rhythm was always there.

Now you know.

Now we begin.

Take one more breath. This one's different from the first. The first breath was recognition. This breath is choice. Breathe in—gathering what you've learned. Breathe out—releasing what no longer serves. That complete cycle? You just did in five seconds what your groups need to remember how to do. Tomorrow, help them remember.

About the Author

Twenty Years Observing How Groups Move, Break, and Heal

D r. Matthew C. Dunn is an organizational psychologist who stumbled into studying group rhythm the way most important discoveries happen—by accident, through failure, and with a lot of confusion.

It began in 2005 with a U14 girls soccer team. As a young coach, he experienced something he couldn't explain: a group that moved, played, and breathed as a single organism. When he couldn't recreate that magic with his next team, he spent the following twenty years trying to understand why some groups sync while others don't, why some spaces feel alive while others suffocate, and why humans are so often exhausted.

With a doctorate in Organizational Leadership Psychology from William James College and five previous books on organizational consciousness and group dynamics, Matthew brought academic rigor to what began as an embodied mystery. Over time, he realized that what groups need isn't more theory—it's permission to trust what their bodies already know.

His journey has taken him from soccer fields to boardrooms, community centers to family dinner tables—watching how the same patterns of exhaustion and vitality show up everywhere humans gather.

Through Field Witness, he works with organizational leaders to recognize and restore natural rhythm—particularly in workplace contexts where violations are most systematic and most exportable. His approach combines pattern recognition, somatic practices, and practical tools for groups ready to move from exhaustion to sustainable flow. Though he's aware that what he observes is shaped by his own position—white, male, educated, economically stable—and that his patterns emerge primarily from post-industrial, digitally-connected contexts where rhythm violations take particular forms.

He is particularly interested in "Field patterns"—the subtle connections and synchronicities that suggest groups exist in potential before they take form. The kind of pattern recognition that lives in bodies before it lives in data.

Matthew lives in Central New York, where he continues to coach (though he's learned not to force magic that isn't there), teaches, navigates family rhythms, and pays attention to how buildings breathe.

His greatest qualification for this book? Twenty years of watching groups suffocate and occasionally—beautifully—remember how to breathe. And one soccer team that taught him everything simply by being exactly what they were: the right nervous systems, at the right time, breathing together.

Quick Rhythm Diagnostic

Your Body Knows Which Pattern Is Stuck

U se this when you feel exhaustion in any group. If multiple patterns are stuck (most are), start with your strongest body signal.

BREATH (Gathering-Dispersing)

Stuck in Chronic GATHERING:

- ☐ Tight chest, shallow breathing
- ☐ Desperate need to be alone
- ☐ Suffocating feeling in groups
- ☐ Meetings that won't end
- ☐ No privacy, always visible
- ☐ Constant group texts/communication
- ☐ Never truly alone
- → *See Chapter 6 for practices*

Stuck in Chronic DISPERSING:

☐ Hollow chest feeling

☐ Reaching sensation, loneliness

☐ Can't connect with others

☐ Groups work in silos

☐ People together but alone

☐ No real meetings or gathering

☐ Isolation despite proximity

→ *See Chapter 6 for practices*

PULSE (Rising-Falling)

Stuck in Chronic RISING:

☐ Racing heart, buzzing nerves

☐ Can't settle or rest

☐ Wired exhaustion, insomnia

☐ Everything urgent/crisis mode

☐ Maximum intensity always

☐ No valleys, only peaks

☐ Burnout approaching or present

→ *See Chapter 6 for practices*

Stuck in Chronic FALLING:

☐ Heavy limbs, no motivation

☐ Emotional flatness

☐ Going through motions

☐ No energy or excitement

☐ Nothing matters feeling

☐ Group has no pulse

☐ Depression-like symptoms

→ *See Chapter 6 for practices*

TIDE (Creating-Dissolving)

Stuck in Chronic CREATING:

☐ Overwhelmed, drowning feeling

☐ Mental congestion

☐ Decision fatigue

☐ Nothing ever completes

☐ Accumulating commitments

☐ 47 committees/projects

☐ Can't let anything go

→ *See Chapter 6 for practices*

Stuck in Chronic DISSOLVING:

☐ Scattered thoughts

☐ Can't focus or build

☐ Ungrounded feeling

☐ Nothing stabilizes

☐ Constant restructuring

☐ High turnover

☐ Nothing sticks

→ *See Chapter 6 for practices*

How to Use:

1. Notice your strongest body signal

2. Match it to a pattern above

3. Name it aloud: "We're stuck in chronic [pattern]"

4. Try one practice from Chapter 6

5. Watch what shifts

Five-Minute Practice Quick Reference

At-a-glance guide when you need a practice quickly.

When BREATH Is Stuck:

If you can't DISPERSE (chronic gathering): -> **Five-Minute Solo:** Step outside alone for five minutes, no phone -> **No-Show Option:** Create guilt-free skip option for gatherings -> **Protected Solo Time:** Designate "dispersing" spots or times

If you can't GATHER (chronic dispersing): -> **Conscious Arrival:** Three seconds eye contact with each person -> **Device-Free Hour:** All phones in box during gathering -> **Gathering Spot:** Create natural convergence point

When PULSE Is Stuck:

If you can't FALL (chronic rising): -> **Empty Saturday:** Nothing scheduled, just existing -> **Valley Hour:** Gentle tasks only—filing, organizing -> **Protected Descent:** After intensity, mandate rest

If you can't RISE (chronic falling): -> **One Good Thing:** Name something that didn't break -> **Two-Minute Music:** Play music that creates movement -> **Stand for What Matters:** Physical rising for important topics

When TIDE Is Stuck:

If you can't DISSOLVE (chronic creating): -> **Gratitude Release:** Thank old pattern and formally release -> **Completion Ceremony:** Mark endings with acknowledgment -> **Sunset Clause:** Everything has expiration date unless renewed

If you can't CREATE (chronic dissolving): -> **Protect One Thing:** One pattern that won't change -> **Name Three Working:** List what works before changing -> **Stable Anchor:** Maintain one consistent rhythm

The Universal Practice:

1. **Notice** - "Something feels stuck"

2. **Name** - Say it aloud to someone

3. **Try** - One practice, 30 seconds minimum

4. **Watch** - Notice what shifts

Remember:

- Not every practice works for every group

- Try one at a time

- Small shifts create large changes

- Your body knows if it's working

- If nothing shifts, see Chapter 6: "When Rhythm Can't Be Restored"

Quick Reference: The Three Movements

BREATH, PULSE, and TIDE Explained

BREATH (Gathering-Dispersing)

The rhythm of coming together and moving apart

When flowing: Groups can gather deeply AND disperse completely. People experience genuine connection without suffocation. Like breathing—inhale and exhale both necessary.

When stuck in chronic gathering: Can't get alone. Constant meetings, forced togetherness, no solitude. Body signals: tight chest, shallow breathing, desperate need to escape.

When stuck in chronic dispersing: Can't connect. Isolated, scattered, no cohesion. Body signals: hollow feeling, loneliness, reaching sensation.

Quick diagnostic: Can this group gather deeply? Can it disperse completely?

See Chapter 4 for full exploration

PULSE (Rising-Falling)

The rhythm of energy intensifying and settling

When flowing: Energy rises and falls naturally. Sustainable engagement. Peak performance followed by genuine rest. Like a heartbeat—both systole and diastole required.

When stuck in chronic rising: Everything urgent, always "on," crisis mode, manic energy. Body signals: racing heart, insomnia, wired but tired, eventual collapse.

When stuck in chronic falling: No energy, flat affect, organizational depression. Body signals: heavy limbs, emotional numbness, can't get started.

Quick diagnostic: Can energy rise naturally here? Can it fall without shame?

See Chapter 4 for full exploration

TIDE (Creating-Dissolving)

The rhythm of things beginning and ending

When flowing: New patterns form while old patterns release. Space for innovation through conscious completion. Natural evolution. Like ocean tides—bringing in and carrying out.

When stuck in chronic creating: Everything accumulates, nothing releases, zombie projects, overwhelming weight. Body signals: drowning feeling, decision fatigue, overwhelm.

When stuck in chronic dissolving: Nothing stabilizes, constant change, no foundation. Body signals: groundlessness, can't focus, scattered thoughts.

Quick diagnostic: Can new things begin here? Can old things end with dignity?

See Chapter 4 for full exploration

Remember

Your body already knows these rhythms. That tight chest is telling you about BREATH violation. That wired exhaustion signals PULSE stuck. That overwhelm indicates TIDE accumulation.

The movements want to flow. They just need you to stop preventing what's already trying to happen.

A Note on Scope

Context and Limitations of These Observations

The patterns in this book emerge from my particular context—largely North American, post-industrial, digitally-connected populations experiencing a specific kind of exhaustion.

I'm a white, cis-gendered man observing mostly professional environments where people have the privilege to worry about "rhythm" rather than survival.

Other communities have different rhythms, different exhaustions, different wisdom. Indigenous communities who never lost their seasonal rhythms might read this and think, "We never forgot how to breathe." Communities facing systemic oppression might say their exhaustion has nothing to do with rhythm and everything to do with injustice.

I offer these observations not as universal truth but as one perspective that might be useful if it resonates with your experience.

Trust what serves you. Leave what doesn't. Your body knows what it needs better than any book.

Five Books That Opened Doors

Further Reading That Shaped These Patterns

These authors explored territory that helped me see patterns. I interpret things through my particular lens, but their work opened doors. Start with whichever calls to your particular curiosity.

1. adrienne maree brown, *Emergent Strategy*

How small shifts create large changes, how fractals work in human systems, how to trust emergence over force. brown shows how collective liberation happens through rhythm and relationship, not through optimization. Her work helped me understand that groups finding their breath might be revolutionary acts. If you want to see how rhythm work connects to justice work, start here.

2. Resmaa Menakem, *My Grandmother's Hands*

How trauma and rhythm live in bodies across generations, particularly racialized trauma that shapes how different communities experience gathering and dispersing. Menakem shows how bodies know things minds deny, how nervous systems carry historical memory, why some groups can't find rhythm because of unmetabolized collective wounds. His work helped me understand that exhaustion might be inherited rhythm violations passed through bodies, and that healing happens somatically, not conceptually.

3. Robin Wall Kimmerer, *Braiding Sweetgrass*

Indigenous wisdom about reciprocity, seasonal rhythms, and what European-descended cultures forgot about living systems. Kimmerer, a botanist and member of the Citizen Potawatomi Nation, shows how plants teach us about gathering and dispersing, creating and dissolving. Her work reminds us that some communities never forgot that life moves in cycles.

4. Christopher Alexander, *A Pattern Language*

Buildings that feel alive versus buildings that feel dead—Alexander mapped the patterns that make the difference. His work revealed that spaces aren't containers but participants, that architecture affects group rhythm, that consciousness might extend through walls. If you've felt how certain spaces help groups breathe while others suffocate, this book explains why.

5. Margaret Wheatley, *Leadership and the New Science*

Organizations as living systems, not machines to optimize. Wheatley brought complexity science to organizational life, showing why control fails, how order emerges from chaos, why groups need freedom to find their form. Her work gave me scientific language for what that first soccer team taught me through pure experience.

A note about reading: Each of these books offers medicine for different kinds of rhythm disruption. You don't need to read them all, or in any particular order. Sometimes one book is exactly what your body needs to hear. Sometimes none of them are right for your context. Trust what calls to you.

These books come from different traditions and contexts. Some will resonate; others won't. Take what serves your context. Honor what doesn't by leaving it where it belongs.

If You Want to Go Deeper

Programs, Resources, and Next Steps

Working With Your Group:

Your body already knows what your group needs. After years observing patterns, the most profound transformations I've witnessed came not from my interventions but from groups recognizing what they already felt. You don't need a consultant to tell you that your team can't breathe or that your family's energy never falls. Your tight chest knows. Your exhausted body knows. Your group's collective wisdom knows.

If you're leading a team, organization, or community ready to explore these patterns together, sometimes having a structured container helps. Not because you need an expert—you are the expert on your own group's experience—but because dedicated time and witnessed practice can accelerate what you already sense. I offer cohort-based programs where groups explore the three movements through their own embodied recognition. I don't teach rhythm; I create space for groups to feel what's already there. These programs simply provide structure for what your body is already trying to tell you.

Learn more at livinggroups.org

For Practitioners:

If you work with groups professionally and these patterns resonate with what you've been observing, you might want language and practices to support what you're already seeing. The exhaustion in your clients' bodies, the stuck patterns in the teams you facilitate—you've been tracking these rhythms even if you didn't have names for them. Training opportunities help practitioners develop pattern recognition skills and share practices, but more importantly, they validate what your embodied cognition has been telling you all along.

Share Your Observations:

If these patterns resonate with your experience—or if they don't—I'd like to hear about it. Not to validate the ideas but to learn what I'm missing.

What patterns do you see that I can't? What exhaustion do you feel that I haven't named? What rhythms does your community know that mine has forgotten?

Website: livinggroups.org
Share patterns: #RhythmOfUs

Field Journal Template

Track Patterns in Your Own Groups

I f you want to track patterns in your own groups, here's a simple structure. Use any notebook—this is just a starting point.

Daily Observations (pick one):

- How did today's BREATH feel? (gathering/dispersing - flowing or stuck?)

- How did today's PULSE feel? (rising/falling - flowing or stuck?)

- How did today's TIDE feel? (creating/dissolving - flowing or stuck?)

- What shifted when I named a pattern?

[Create your own 30-day grid or use any notebook]

Weekly Reflection:

- Which groups felt alive this week?

- Where did I notice stuck patterns?

- What rhythm did my body need that it didn't get?

- What small shift might I try next week?

If tracking helps you notice patterns, use it. If it feels like another task, skip it. Your body knows what it needs.

Final Words

One Breath at a Time

T wenty years ago, a soccer team taught me that groups are alive. Since then, I've been trying to understand what that means.

This book is my current understanding. It's incomplete, culturally limited, and probably wrong about some things.

But if it helps you trust what your body already knows, if it gives you permission to name what feels off, if it lets you make one small adjustment toward a rhythm that serves life—then it's done its work.

The rhythm was always there. Now you might have words for it.

Use them carefully. Share them gently. Let them change as they need to.

The revolution isn't in the ideas. It's in the recognition. Especially in workplaces—where rhythm violations are most systematic—recognition might be the beginning of transformation that ripples everywhere.

One breath at a time.

Dr. Matthew C. Dunn
2025

Breathe

This is us